Another...

The Same Kind, but Different

by

James A. Rushton

Another...: The Same Kind, but Different
Copyright © 2004 by James Rushton
ISBN: 09762744-0-X

Published by: James A. Rushton Ministries
P.O. Box 256, Ocean Gate, New Jersey 08740

Printing: Fidlar Doubleday

Cover design: Joy Hirschy
Word of Life Church, Dubuque, Iowa

Editorial services: Daiscia Roseberry
KTT Publishing, located at *www.knowthetruthministries.com*.

To my precious wife and son-- and to you the reader of this book. May reading the content of these pages bring you clearer awareness of the Greater One within you.

CONTENTS

Another…: The Same Kind, but Different

JUST FOR YOU

Just for you, Jesus was . . .
Sent from God.
Born of a virgin.
Nailed to the cross.
Raised from the dead.

Just for you, Jesus is . . .
Your Righteousness.
Your Peace.
Your Good Shepherd.
Your Friend.
Your Victory.
Your Healer.
Your Provider.

Just for you, Jesus asked the Father to send...
Another Comforter, called the Holy Ghost.

Just for you, the Holy Spirit came and is. . .
Your Comforter.
Your Helper.
Your Standby
Your Counselor.
Your Strengthener.
Your Intercessor.
Your Advocate.

Another...: The Same Kind, but Different

A PERSONAL WORD

This book is about the Holy Spirit. Certainly, there is much to be said and learned about all the things of God. Many books have already been written about the Holy Spirit, and I'm sure many more will be written. Books have even been written to address praying in the Spirit, or in tongues—but nothing has been thorough enough to adequately convey the power and wisdom available to those who will take full advantage of praying in this manner. You will notice in the back of this book that there is a list of 28 reasons for praying in tongues—read them, study them, and add them to your life.

Over the span of years that has comprised my Christian life, I have come to realize that I need all the help I can get from the Holy Spirit. Without the Holy Spirit, I would be nothing and would do nothing. Yes, I know that without Jesus, I would be nothing—yet, as a born-again believer, I'm not without Him. And, without the Father, there would be nothing—yet He exists and has already created everything. But just think about it... You could hear every nuance of the Word with your physical ears—but without the Holy Spirit to reveal them and bring manifestation, those truths would never produce in your life. And it is this very Holy Spirit that is so often overlooked or blatantly rejected.

It is true that Jesus sent His Word and saved, healed, and delivered—but it takes the Holy Spirit to *reveal* that Word, and it takes your believing to receive it. And, the Holy Spirit's involvement is not limited to revealing the Word—after the promise or plan has been revealed and you stand in faith, the Holy Spirit moves to cause it to manifest.

Maybe you are in a situation right now where you need to receive something from God or to do something for Him—but nothing has materialized. *The hindrance could be that you have not allowed the Holy Spirit all the freedom He needs to bring these things to pass.* The Lord is saying the same thing to us as He said to Zerubbabel through Zechariah in Zechariah 4:6: *"...Not by might, nor by power, but by my spirit...."*

Like Jesus, we must be in the condition and position to be and do all God has for us. And just like Jesus, we need the Holy Spirit—not only as Teacher, as a Guide, or to help with manifestation, but also as our Comforter, Helper, Standby, Strengthener, Intercessor, and Advocate. So, my friend, let Him be all these things to you, for you, and with you.

It is my prayer that what you learn within this book will help you to be and to do all God has for you—for His glory and for your benefit.

> *Praise be to the God and Father of our Lord Jesus Christ, the Father of compassion and the God of all comfort, who comforts us in all our troubles, so that we can comfort those in any trouble with the comfort we ourselves have received from God* (2 Corinthians 1:3-4, *NIV*).

> *I will pray the Father, and he shall give you another Comforter, that he may abide with you for ever; Even the Spirit of truth; whom the world cannot receive, because it seeth him not, neither knoweth him: but ye know him;*

for he dwelleth with you, and shall be in you (John 14:16-17).

Another...: The Same Kind, but Different

INTRODUCTION

As we approach this study of the Holy Spirit as Another Comforter, please keep forefront in your mind that He can be Another Comforter to you in any area of your life. And, don't receive Him just for you, but let Him flow through you to others. Remember, Jesus said that the Holy Spirit would empower us to be witnesses: *"But ye shall receive power, after that the Holy Ghost is come upon you: and ye shall be witnesses unto me both in Jerusalem, and in all Judaea, and in Samaria, and unto the uttermost part of the earth"* (Acts 1:8).

Jesus said in John 18:37 37, *"...to this end was I born, and for this cause came I into the world, that I should bear witness unto the truth."* This is one of the reasons *you* were re-born—and the Holy Spirit desires to help you accomplish this. He does so personally, through your fellowship with Him, and outwardly, through the ministry gifts (e.g., apostles, prophets, evangelists, pastors, and teachers) that He has placed within the Church.

First, we need to hear and receive the Word of God so that we will *have* the truth. Then, we need to bear witness, or testify, of that truth with our words and actions. Once we do, the Holy Spirit acknowledges the presence of that truth in our lives by producing for us and influencing the lives of others through us. But, remember, the Holy Spirit is a Helper, and He can't help you if you do not grant Him permission.

The Holy Spirit has a work to do, so let Him do it! The Word has a work to do in your life—let it perform it. You know what the word *work* means? It means, "a transfer of energy that occurs when a force makes something move" (I learned this in science class). Please note that believing *is* work. When we hear the Word, believe the Word, and speak the Word, it produces the very energy that prompts the Holy Spirit to move for us just as He moved for God when God created the heavens, the earth, and man (Genesis 1).

We have energy to believe and speak. The words that we speak are creative energy. The Holy Spirit has energy. When these energies are released, something moves. But guess what? *We* are the ones who have the authority to "start things rolling." The movement you find around you comes from the words that you release. Just as words of faith from God's Word move all of heaven on your behalf, words of fear, the flesh, or of the Devil's kingdom will put your flesh and demonic forces into action. So let the show begin in *faith*: action, please!

One of the words we need to become familiar with is *inspire*. When we look at this word, it leads us to another important word, which is *influence*. *Webster's New World Dictionary of the American Language* gives the following definitions:

> To *inspire* means "to breathe, to influence, stimulate, or impel, as to some creative or effective effort; to guide or motivate by divine influence; to cause to be said or written."

> *Influence* is "the power of persons or things to affect others and the effect of such power."

These two words greatly affect our walk with the Lord in the Spirit. For us to walk in the Spirit, we need the Word of God and the Holy Spirit to inspire us. Then, we must take the next step to release the truths of God's Word that inspired us and use them to positively influence others. What's the use of being inspired with the things of God if you never do anything with them? It is essential to share them. They will return to you by the power of the Holy Spirit and be a blessing to you and others—this is called *bearing witness of the truth.*

You know and I know that the Devil comes *"...to steal, and to kill, and to destroy..."* (John 10:10). He is always trying to influence us. Why? To keep us from being inspired by the people and the things of God so that we will not be good witnesses. And he's not the only culprit. The flesh is always warring against our spirits, trying to pull us in its direction.

For us to be a positive influence, we must first be inspired by the Word of God and the Holy Spirit so much that we begin to say and write the things of God. That is why I am writing this book. That is why I speak the Word of God. You are not the only one I want to influence—I want to influence the Holy Spirit so that He starts saying and doing things on my behalf. As I breathe in the things of God, they inspire me—causing me to speak forth the things of God and, thereby, drawing blessings to others as well as to me.

The Word has a work to do. The Holy Spirit has a work to do. We have a work to do. Each of us has something to accomplish that will fail if we do not allow the Word and the Holy Spirit to work. Our responsibility is to be inspired by the things of God until they influence our speech and actions. Then we are to take that inspiration and use it to influence circumstances and others. Jesus did both. He inspired and influenced people, both dead and alive; and He influenced things like storms, water, fish, and bread, as well as sickness and disease.

There was a point when I was a missionary to the Philippines where I became so fed up that I decided to quit. I began to pack up and intended to go home. I will never forget what the Holy Spirit said to me: *"You have a job to do, but you've been acting like you don't need My help. You need to start cooperating with Me."* How do we get to a place where we are cooperating with Him? By ceasing our vain efforts to do things in our own strength and by allowing Him to breathe on us. I pray that you begin to allow the Holy Spirit to breathe the things of God on you.

Please understand, I am not writing this as one who has completely "arrived," but as one who has not quit and desires to better serve God. We need the Comforter every day in every area. So, let the Holy Spirit do His work completely in every area of your life.

♦ ♦ ♦ ♦ ♦ ♦ ♦

Ye are of God, little children, and have overcome them: because greater is he that is in you than he that is in the world
(1 John 4:4).

1

GOD USED THE HOLY SPIRIT

God used His Words, but needed the Holy Spirit: *"In the beginning God created the heavens and the earth. Now the earth was formless and empty, darkness was over the surface of the deep, and the Spirit of God was hovering over the waters"* (Genesis 1:1-2, *NIV*).

One of the responsibilities of the Holy Spirit is to help bring forth the things of God on this earth. I use the words *bring forth,* because all things were created by Jesus; but, it is one of the responsibilities of the Holy Spirit to bring forth, or deliver, the things of God. Remember that it takes faith. In the beginning, God looked out over the earth and saw that there was darkness and a void over the earth. Being that He is the God that He is, He does not like darkness or things being void. So, God decided to do something about it. But, God needed some help. Let us remember, the "Big Three" were there all along: God the Father, the Word, and the Holy Spirit. Many years after this, the Word became flesh and lived with and as one of us. When He did this, He was called Jesus (John 1:1-3, 14):

> *In the beginning was the Word, and the Word was with God, and the Word was God. The same was in the beginning with God. All things were made by him; and without him was not any thing made that was made. And the Word was made flesh, and dwelt among us, (and we beheld his glory, the glory as of the only begotten of the Father,) full of grace and truth.*

About 33 years after the Word became flesh, the Holy Spirit was asked to come and make Himself available to help us.

You can see in Genesis 1:2 that the Holy Spirit was hovering over the earth. Why was He just hovering? Why was He not taking action? Because God had not yet asked Him to help. At that time, He was standing by God, standing by the Word—He was doing His job. Please understand, the Holy Spirit did not and does not have to help God in the same way that He helps us. He does not need to be a Teacher to God, nor does He need to be Another Comforter to God; but, He is the One Who helps God get things done.

Ever Ready to Help

Now think about this... The Holy Spirit's job has not changed; He is just doing it for people. He is still hovering over places of darkness and wherever there is a void. Why? Because the Father, Son, and Holy Spirit do not like darkness or places that are void of life! They are always making themselves available to do whatever is necessary to fill the voids and to displace the darkness in peoples' lives.

Darkness resides in people who are outside the family of God. Those in the family of God can have voids, or empty places, in their lives as a result of not allowing God's Word and the Holy Spirit to continue moving. The Holy Spirit is hovering, in readiness to help even as you read this book. Just as in the beginning with God, He is with and over *you*.

Yes, as born-again believers, He is *in* us; but He wants to do things *for* us. He desires to expose darkness and those hollow places and displace them with His light. He wants to guide us into all truth so that He can teach us—and we can be free. He desires that every place there is something missing or empty in our lives—whether mental, physical (in body or finances), or spiritual—to be completely filled, or made whole.

In Genesis 1:1-3, God saw the darkness and void and made a decision to do something about it:

> *In the beginning God created the heaven and the earth. And the earth was without form, and void; and darkness was upon the face of the deep. And the Spirit of God moved upon the face of the waters. And God said, Let there be light: and there was light.*

Why did He use His Word? Because He wanted to set the stage for the Holy Spirit to move. How? By speaking His words in love and by faith. Why do I say this? Because God is love, and He is a faith God.

You can read the rest of the creation story in Genesis and see that God continued speaking and setting the stage for each and every thing He wanted accomplished. When one project was finished, He would stop talking until He wanted to do something else. Thank God that He said many more things and that each and everything He said was for you and me—so we could be complete and no longer empty or lacking.

The Father did not try to do it all alone. He allowed the Word and Holy Spirit to do their jobs. He cooperated with the Word, and the Holy Spirit cooperated with the Word—and the results were the removal of darkness and the filling of the void.

Set the Stage

Notice that when God wanted light, He *said,* "Light, be." When He wanted waters together, He *said,* "Waters, be together," and they were so. Take time to read Genesis 1. I suggest to you that if there are dark or empty places in your life, get the Word on the scene. Open your mouth—set the stage for the Holy Spirit to move! But you must do so by faith and in love. Do not just *say* you love God, but *prove* it by walking in faith.

Just as He did in the beginning with creation, the Holy Spirit is hovering over the darkness and voids of *your* life, just waiting to move. He's just waiting for you to speak the Word. *Do you see that when God saw the darkness and void over the earth, He took on the responsibility to do something about it? Why did He do this? Because it was His, and He wanted to restore it.*

The earth could not call on the Lord to save it and to remove its darkness and fill its voids. But, bless God, you and I can! *We have the responsibility of positioning ourselves for the Holy Spirit to move—and to help others take responsibility to do the same.* I'll say it again: the Holy Spirit is hovering over the darkness and voids of your life and of others. He is just waiting for someone to speak the Word and set the stage for Him to perform. Do you know what happens when He performs? He delivers the blessings, wisdom, and manifestations of God!

Let His Spirit Guide You

You may not know where to start or what to say. This is where the Holy Spirit can help. Once you're in position, He will guide you into all truth and teach you what to say for your own personal growth and instruct you in what to confess over and for yourself and others.

Maybe you have heard Kenneth E. Hagin's testimony of how he was healed and raised from his deathbed when he was a teenager. I thank God that this man was used so mightily for the kingdom. I also thank God that his teachings are still being used today to help millions learn how to live by faith and to know their authority in Christ and through the use of His name— authority made available to them because of Jesus' great love and sacrifice.

Allow me to bring something to your attention: it was the Holy Spirit that led Kenneth E. Hagin into the truth of Mark 11:23, and it was the Holy Spirit that taught him that truth and how to use it. It was knowing, understanding, believing, and properly applying that truth that made Brother Hagin whole and brought about the complete manifestation of his healing.

Note: There are not many people who believe, receive, and walk in a truth from God's Word the first time they hear it. *Walking in truth requires your looking for it. It also takes the Holy Spirit to reveal it, to teach you how to walk in it, and to guide you in how, when, and where to use the truth that was revealed to you.*

Certainly, we are to keep a positive confession of God's Word. This helps us maintain a good and blessed life. At the same time, we know there are times when the Enemy attacks us with the things of his kingdom. It is in these times that we need to go beyond relying on the Word alone and begin trusting in the Holy Spirit to lead us to victory. We can know all the scriptures there are, but it takes the Holy Spirit to direct us to the correct ones to apply to specific situations and to alert us to any personal adjustments that we may need to make.

There have only been a few times in my life that I have been ill; and in each of these instances, I successfully maintained a good confession. However, I needed more than a good confession to bring about the results I needed—I needed the Holy Spirit.

One time, I was reading the Bible on the way to a ministry meeting (someone else was driving), and the Enemy struck a blow with a force like a bomb. The end result was a head-on collision. I was rushed to the hospital and was not expected to live. Many things were broken and damaged in my body. Throughout this ordeal, I continued my confessions and prayed—even so, I still hurt. Then, one night, the Holy Spirit spoke to me and instructed me to have communion. I heeded His direction and asked someone to come. During the breaking of the bread and drinking from the cup in remembrance of Jesus, the healing, hurt-removing power of God went through my body.

I recall another time when I experienced such excruciating pain from kidney stones that Mary had to call 9-1-1. I prayed and confessed all I knew about healing. Even so, this mighty man of faith and power was on the floor and unable to move as the ambulance approached with its red lights flashing and the sound of its siren ringing through the air.

After arriving at the hospital and lying in the Emergency Room, the Holy Spirit told me to, "Pray in the Spirit loudly." I did so, and the kidney stones left and have never returned. Not only that, but a technician heard my praying in tongues, recognized the words as Latin, and relayed to another hospital staff member that I was giving God the highest praise! Imagine that—I was praying in tongues, but someone else heard my prayers as praise to God in Latin!

Another time, after coming home from teaching a Bible class, the Enemy struck me with a very high fever. My temperature was over 103 degrees for two days. Needless to say, I prayed.

Mary prayed. We quoted the Scriptures. We used the name of Jesus—but nothing seemed to be happening. Things were not looking good, so I said, "Lord, I do not know what else to say or do."

When you are experiencing a very high temperature, there is not much you can do except to speak and listen. I had been using my mouth, but then I decided to be quiet so that I could hear what the Spirit was saying. He told me to forgive someone and to ask Jesus to forgive that person as well. Just as soon as I did, the fever departed.

Remain Teachable

Yes, we are to learn the truths in God's Word. Jesus certainly did, but guess what? Jesus only said and did what the Father wanted Him to say and do.

Remember, before Jesus ever started in the ministry—and even before He was empowered by the Holy Spirit—He had already increased in wisdom, stature, and in favor with God and man (Luke 2:52). That is why He could be used in such a powerful way. Jesus had something in Him for the Holy Spirit to work with. One more thing: the reason that the Devil could not use Jesus was that there was nothing in Jesus for the Devil to use. He was the Word in heaven, and that Word became flesh and dwelt among us.

In the beginning was the Word, and the Word was with God, and the Word was God (John 1: 1).

And the Word was made flesh, and dwelt among us, (and we beheld his glory, the glory as of the only begotten of the Father,) full of grace and truth (John 1:14).

Even with all He was before, He still had to grow in the wisdom and stature of God when He took on the form of man. Because Jesus had become a man, He did this by filling Himself with the Word and by depending totally on the Holy Spirit to know what, how, and when to say something—and even, sometimes, when not to say anything at all.

> *Howbeit when he, the Spirit of truth, is come, he will guide you into all truth: for he shall not speak of himself; but whatsoever he shall hear, that shall he speak: and he will shew you things to come* (John 16:13).

If you will put yourself in a position to be taught and purpose to remain teachable, the Holy Spirit *will* bring the things of God to your remembrance:

> *But the Comforter, which is the Holy Ghost, whom the Father will send in my name, he shall teach you all things, and bring all things to your remembrance, whatsoever I have said unto you* (John 14:26).

> *For the Holy Spirit will teach you at that time what you should say* (Luke 12:12, *NIV*).

I have a charge to myself and to you: *Get full of the Word and allow the Holy Spirit to teach you the how's, when's, and where's.* He will do this for you so that you can have a very successful personal life and so that you may be a blessing to others. In my personal life, I have found this to be true, and it still amazes me how often He will bring things to my remembrance and show me how to use them to help others: *Thus saith the LORD, thy Redeemer, the Holy One of Israel; I am the LORD thy God which teacheth thee to profit, which leadeth thee by the way that thou shouldest go* (Isaiah 48:17).

Notice some of the words used in the last few scriptures: *guide*, *show*, *teach*, *remembrance*, and *lead*. These words are very important in our relationship with the Holy Spirit. To set the stage for the Holy Spirit to perform, all of these words must come into play. You must be guided into the truth. The Spirit must lead you. Once you have been guided to the truth, you must allow Him to teach it to you. And, you must keep it in your heart so that He can bring it to your remembrance.

My wife and I were missionaries in the Philippines for over twelve years. We were led to go there. After we responded to the leading of the Spirit to go, He guided us on how to get there. And, after we arrived, we had to be taught how to live there.

We were led by the Spirit to become children of God, and we were guided into the truth on how to do so. Yet even after that, we had to be taught how to live in His family; we had to be taught how to live in His kingdom here on the earth.

Remember, we cannot live here the way He desires based on just one truth from His Word. We need to always put ourselves in a position to be guided into more truth. And, we must be taught how to walk in that truth under the direction of the Holy Spirit.

You know what is so amazing? God knows this, Jesus knows this, and the Holy Spirit knows this. That is why they did three distinct things to help us in these areas. First, they sent the Holy Spirit. Then they gave us ministry gifts (Ephesians 4:11-15):

And he gave some, apostles; and some, prophets; and some, evangelists; and some, pastors and teachers; For the perfecting of the saints, for the work of the ministry, for the edifying of the body of Christ: Till we all come in the unity of the faith, and of the knowledge of the Son of God, unto a perfect man, unto the measure of the stature of the fulness of Christ: That we henceforth be no more children, tossed to and fro, and carried about with every wind of doctrine, by the sleight of men, and cunning craftiness, whereby they lie in wait to deceive; But speaking the truth in love, may grow up into him in all things, which is the head, even Christ....

And, finally, They gave us each other. Do you realize that when you fellowship with others of like special faith, they help you with the things of God? We should live our lives so that the things of God will be added to our lives and to the lives of those around us.

Just think about it. How many truths are there in the Word of God that we need to be guided to and taught how to use? These truths are not for us to just hear. We are to act on them. We start the movement of the Spirit by the speaking of our mouths.

♦ ♦ ♦ ♦ ♦ ♦ ♦

The Holy Spirit will help you as He leads and guides you into truth. Then, He will teach you how to walk in it.

But be ye doers of the word, and not hearers only, deceiving your own selves (James 1:22).

2

FELLOWSHIP

The grace of the Lord Jesus Christ, and the love of God, and the communion of the Holy Ghost, be with you all (2 Corinthians 13:14).

That which we have seen and heard declare we unto you, that ye also may have fellowship with us: and truly our fellowship is with the Father, and with his Son Jesus Christ (1 John 1:3).

If we say that we have fellowship with him, and walk in darkness, we lie, and do not the truth... (1 John 1:6).

But if we walk in the light, as he is in the light, we have fellowship one with another, and the blood of Jesus Christ his Son cleanseth us from all sin (1 John 1:7).

♦ ♦ ♦ ♦ ♦ ♦ ♦

We are not to have fellowship with darkness. You can see in the scriptures listed above that there are four things with which we are to have fellowship: the Father, the Son, the Holy Spirit, and one another.

If we emphasize one of these and leave the others out, we will be off balance and "run into the ditch." To keep us upright, we need all four; and, as you will see, each one does something special in our lives.

To better understand and to know the Father, the Son, the Holy Spirit, and each other, we must spend time with each. To get to know the first three, you invest time reading the Bible—listening, pondering, and praying God's Word. The more you learn the Word, the more you will learn about the Father, Jesus, the Holy Spirit, and your brothers and sisters in Christ.

What It Means to Know

Just because you have been introduced to someone does not mean you *know* him or her. Mary said to the angel, *"For I do not know a man"* (Luke 1:34). Yet, she was already engaged to Joseph. After Jesus' arrest, Peter denied knowing Jesus three times—even though he had walked closely with Jesus for a total of about three years. Why? Unlike in today's society, to say in biblical times that you *knew* someone was to convey a relationship deeper than merely one of acquaintance—it implied intimacy, or closeness.

I have been introduced to many people I do not know in this way. I may know their name or what they do for a living, but to say I *know* them? I don't. What does *know* mean? It means, "to have a close working relationship—one that produces fruit as you work with."

You do not need to know every minor detail about someone to produce fruit—but you do need to know something deeper than a name. In order to become born again, you had to know more than just Jesus' name: you realized that you would be saved if you called upon His name. Guess what! The more you know the Father, Jesus, and the Holy Spirit, the better the fruit will be—and it will be fruit that will last.

True Fellowship

How or what must we do to come to a point of truly knowing someone? Through fellowship with the person we desire to know. It may not be always about spiritual things, either. Fellowship is also needed to run a job and to keep relationships healthy. What must we do to have fellowship? It takes time, time, and more time! But to turn it from just time spent to true fellowship—for it to be complete and come to point of producing fruit—there are three things we must do:

1. *Recognize* the other person

   Of course, you can recognize someone physically, but that is not fellowship. With physical recognition, you could still choose to turn the other way. To truly recognize someone, you must *give the person time to speak.* Just because you give them time to speak does not make it fellowship—you still need the other two actions. For example, husbands are experts at recognizing their wives to the point of just letting them speak. Many homes are fruitless, because there is only a bunch of talking. Remember, no fellowship equals no fruit. It takes more than giving someone time to speak. You must also...

2. *Receive* the other person

   First, you must give the other person time to speak, as we mentioned; but you must also *listen to and receive what the person is saying.*

   I would suggest you listen with your eyes and ears and allow your interest to show by the expression on your face. Your countenance shows if you are really listening, which brings us to the third thing that must be involved for fellowship to be complete...

3. *Enjoy* the other person

This means that you *take pleasure in being with the person.* We all have been guilty of saying or acting like we are engaging in fellowship, but doing so with no enjoyment— and then we wonder what is wrong. It may be as simple as our not having our act together to fellowship in the things of God.

There are other things involved, but it takes these three in operation for it to be genuine fellowship. How can you learn to be like someone if you do not fellowship? How can you get to love each other to the fullest if you do not fellowship? It is best we apply these words to the Father, the Word, the Holy Spirit, and those of like precious faith, as well as to your family.

Have No Fellowship with Darkness

It's sad to say, but these same principles work in the Devil's kingdom. That dark kingdom has its own so-called apostles, prophets, evangelists, pastors, teachers, helpers, and witnesses.

The Word of God very clearly warns us to have no fellowship with darkness at all: *"But I say, that the things, which the Gentiles sacrifice, they sacrifice to devils, and not to God: and I would not that ye should have fellowship with devils"* (1 Corinthians 10:20). Ephesians 5:11 confirms this and further instructs us to reprove them: *"And have no fellowship with the unfruitful works of darkness, but rather reprove them."*

Some of the definitions of *reprove* are, "to convict, refute, confute; by conviction to bring to the light, to expose; to find fault with, correct by word; to reprehend severely; to call to account, show one his fault." More plainly, this means you speak your disapproval of devils and fleshly ways. You cannot reprove without speaking. Keeping silent does not get the job done when it comes to the Devil's ways. You must say something—expose the darkness; expose, call to account, and correct it with the light of God's Word that you speak!

Do you know how people come to a point where they are involved with the things of the Devil? They start fellowshipping with things of his kingdom. They don't stop at just letting them speak (through thoughts, media, written materials, and ungodly people)—even though they probably realize what they're hearing is wrong. No, they start receiving, listening to and considering what the Enemy is saying. Then they start enjoying it—that is when they become "hooked."

The fall of mankind came, because Adam and Eve began fellowshipping with the Devil. It does not take much time of fellowship for those you are with to have an affect on you. Many times it can be one look or one word. If we recognize, receive, and enjoy something, we will probably do it—unless we come to realize it is wrong and repent.

A Better Way

Choose instead to recognize, receive, and enjoy all the things of God. Recognize, receive, and enjoy the reading and studying of His Word. Recognize, receive, and enjoy the Holy Spirit as your Teacher, Guide, and Leader. Do these things even when they may not be comfortable. According to 2 Timothy 3:16, *"All scripture is given by inspiration of God, and is profitable for doctrine, for reproof, for correction, for instruction in righteousness."* Look closely at this verse—notice that each thing God's Word does helps us to *be* better and to *do* better. His Word is *profitable*:

1. As it is inspired, or God-breathed, it motivates us.
2. For doctrine, His guidelines for becoming Christ-like and adding understanding to our lives.
3. For reproof—it lets us know what God disapproves of in our lives.
4. For correction, for it replaces the errors in our lives with truth.
5. For instruction in righteousness, teaching us how to do things God's way.

Override the Flesh

Don't let your flesh determine your fellowship. If you do, it will get you in trouble. There are many things the flesh recognizes, receives, and enjoys that will cause you trouble if they are not tempered with the Word of God.

For example, your flesh wants sex. Do you realize fellowship is involved with sex? But the Bible tells us sex should be reserved for the marriage bed, between a man and woman only. The act of two people of the same gender having sex with each other is sin. Sex outside of the marriage covenant is sin.

Another thing your flesh desires is food, but what and how much you eat must be under discipline. The Holy Spirit will help you with this if you ask Him to help. He knows your body better than you do.

Other things the flesh recognizes, receives, and enjoys are listed in Galatians 5:19-21: *"Now the works of the flesh are manifested, which are these...."* Let me interrupt here and bring your attention to two words here: *works* and *manifested*. For these works to manifest, fellowship had to be taking place. Again, Galatians 5:19-21 says:

> *Now the works of the flesh are manifest, which are these; Adultery, fornication, uncleanness, lasciviousness, Idolatry, witchcraft, hatred, variance, emulations, wrath, strife, seditions, heresies, Envyings, murders, drunkenness, revellings, and such like: of the which I tell you before, as I have also told you in time past, that they which do such things shall not inherit the kingdom of God.*

The last part of this verse tells us the consequence of fellowship with the things of the flesh: Fellowship with the flesh, and you will not inherit the kingdom of God.

Instead, as 1 Peter 4:1 reveals, we are to have the same mind as Christ, who endured persecution and temptation instead of giving in to the flesh: *"Forasmuch then as Christ hath suffered for us in the flesh, arm yourselves likewise with the same mind: for he that hath suffered in the flesh hath ceased from sin."* It is the flesh that suffers when we allow God's Word by the Holy Spirit to have its way in our lives. Simply put, the flesh does not like the things of God (Galatians 5:17): *"For the flesh lusteth against the Spirit, and the Spirit against the flesh: and these are contrary the one to the other: so that ye cannot do the things that ye would."*

How do we get to the point that our flesh is not having its way? Look at the first part of 1 Peter 4:1, *"...arm yourselves with the mind of Christ."* If we keep allowing the things of God to have free rein, the flesh will be overruled—and you will have complete victory. So, just tell your flesh to "be quiet." *Let your mind be in agreement with the Word of God. As your spirit flows with the Holy Spirit, you will rule over your flesh.*

"This I say then, Walk in the Spirit, and ye shall not fulfill the lust of the flesh" (Galatians 5:16). *"If we live in the Spirit, let us also walk in the Spirit"* (Galatians 5:25). *Walking in the Spirit* is minding the things of God more than we mind the things of the flesh. Just think about it: if we mind the things of God more than the flesh, we will walk in love and faith.

Fellowship with the Word

Why the Word? There are many reasons for our needing the Word. We need to focus here on wanting the Word, because true fellowship must be based on God's Word. Why? The Word shows us Jesus in operation—and when we see Jesus, we see the Father. When a person truly gives the Word first place, that brings the Holy Spirit on the scene. When the Holy Spirit shows up, He reveals more of Jesus.

What you're about to read is extremely important... *If you do not recognize, receive, and enjoy the Word, it will be very difficult for you to see Jesus, the Father, the Holy Spirit, and all they have done and made available to you.*

Sometimes I think it would have been nice if God had written the Word in three distinct volumes: one on Him as the Father, one on Him as the Word, and one on Him as the Holy Spirit. Then He could have given us other volumes covering all the things He has for us to be, do, and receive.

But that would not have worked, because I would probably pick one I liked better than the others, only to leave the others out. People do this even though it is all in one book. They pick and choose their favorite scriptures, favorite books, and favorite men and women in the Bible. I went to school with a guy that loved King David and knew more about him than any other person or thing in the Bible. Others have loved Jesus more than the Father. Others have loved the Holy Spirit and tongues more than anything else.

It kind of reminds me of a cookbook—a general cookbook, not just one for desserts. Everything in the book is good, but we tend to just pick and major on one or two things we like. When we do this with the Word of God, it hinders our growing up and maturing in a Christ-like way. We must fellowship with the Word of God and allow the Holy Spirit to move in our hearts, minds, and bodies. Remember the Word of God includes water, oil, milk, and meat with desserts.

You know why God did not allow the Bible to be printed in many volumes? Because He wanted us to see it is a unit and to take it as a whole. He said in 2 Timothy 3:16, *"All scripture...."* *All* means all, all, all, and all! The entirety of Scripture gives you a complete picture of Jesus, a complete picture of the Father, a complete picture of the Holy Spirit, and a complete picture of you! It gives a complete picture of what you are to be and do, as well as a complete understanding of how the flesh and the Devil operate. If you desire to learn these things, fellowship with the Word of God.

Hebrews 1:3 (*AMP*) states very clearly that Jesus is the express image of the Father:

> *"He is the sole expression of the glory of God [the Light-being, the out-raying or radiance of the divine],*

and He is the perfect imprint and very image of [God's] nature, upholding and maintaining and guiding and propelling the universe by His mighty word of power. When He had by offering Himself accomplished our cleansing of sins and riddance of guilt, He sat down at the right hand of the divine Majesty on high."

So we can very clearly see that if we know the Word, not just a few promises, we will see a picture of Jesus. When you see Jesus, you have seen the Father (John 14:7-9).

The Influence of Fellowship

Another reason fellowship is important and valuable is that *whatever we have fellowship with will influence us—and what influences us will cause us to influence others.* Remember, this works both with positive and negative things. So, let us determine to allow the Word of God, by the Holy Spirit, to influence us as we fellowship with the things of God. The following scriptures demonstrate that we grow and mature into Christ-likeness as we fellowship with the Word of God.

And as we have borne the image of the man of dust, we shall also bear the image of the heavenly Man (1 Corinthians 15:49, *NKJV*).

For whom he did foreknow, he also did predestinate to be conformed to the image of his Son, that he might be the firstborn among many brethren (Romans 8:29).

But we all, with open face beholding as in a glass the glory of the Lord, are changed into the same image from glory to glory, even as by the Spirit of the Lord (2 Corinthians 3:18, *NKJV*).

◆◆◆◆◆◆◆

As we choose the Father, the Son, and the Holy Spirit as our source of fellowship, our destiny is Christ-likeness.

◆◆◆◆◆

Then they that feared the LORD spoke often one to another: and the LORD hearkened, and heard it, and a book of remembrance was written before him for them that feared the LORD, and that thought upon his name (Malachi 3:16).

3

AN ENCOUNTER WITH JESUS

In November 1969, I had come to a point in my life where I did not want to live like I was living anymore. I came home one night at one o'clock in the morning and lay down on the bed. I told God I did not know Him and that I wanted to die, because I did not want to live like I was living anymore.

I lay there for a while and then went to sleep. About an hour later, I thought I heard someone knocking on the front door of the house. Upset that someone had the nerve to awake me at this hour, I started toward the door to give someone a "piece of my mind" and a "knuckle breakfast."

I took two steps and ran right into Jesus. I literally bumped into Him, for He was standing in the doorway of my bedroom. He was just as clear to me as anything in this room is to me right now.

After bumping into Jesus, I fell to the floor. The next thing I knew, I was sitting on the floor beside the bed, looking straight into the face and eyes of Jesus. His eyes looked like lakes of fire consuming me, but His eyes were also full of concern for me—full of compassion and love.

As I looked up unto His eyes and face, He reached down to me with both hands to lift me up. As He was doing this, He said these words to me:

> *Jimmy, I love you, and I saved you for something. Pick up your Bible and follow me. I have called you to prepare yourself for my ministry. You will not see me like this any more as long as you live on the face of this earth.*

I would like to take the time to share on some of the words Jesus said to me that night.

"I Love You"

He said, *"Jimmy, I love you."* This is the heartbeat of Jesus. He loves you. He loved the world so much that He obeyed the Father and gave His life for you and me. But, you know, love is not complete until both people involved receive it. God loves you—and if you have not received His love, do so right now!

Another thing about this love of God is that for it to continue to be of any benefit to you, you must continue in it. Let Him by His Word and His Spirit love you the way He desires to love you. Allow Him to teach you how to love Him and to love others. This is something all of us need everyday of our lives.

"I Saved You for Something"

He said, *"I saved you for something."* What? To be His child and develop until I can be called a mature son and mind the Father's business. You can see clearly from the Scriptures that we are to grow and develop to be more like Jesus.

Not only did Jesus save me so that I could grow up in Him and become a full-grown son, He saved me so that, after I grew up and matured in Him, I could mind His business and do His work. Do you know what is so wonderful about all this? As we grow and do His work, our joy becomes full. That is why He wants us to do His desires—so that our joy will be full (John 15:11).

Everything Father, Jesus, and the Holy Spirit ask us to do is always for our benefit first. Even calling on the name of the Lord is for your benefit first. *Only after you are benefited by the new birth are you able to be of benefit to someone else.* Our being baptized with the Holy Spirit and speaking in tongues is for our benefit first. As we allow the Holy Spirit to comfort us, to help us, to strengthen us, to stand by us, to be our Advocate and to be our Intercessor, then we can be of benefit to God and to someone else.

"Pick Up Your Bible"

He said, *"Pick up your Bible."* When Jesus finished saying these words to me, I said, "Lord I don't have a Bible." He said, *"Yes you do—look under the bed."* It is amazing how quick we are to tell Jesus what we do not have when we heard what He just said. I should have realized that when Jesus tells you to pick up something, it means it is there and that you can.

There was something very amazing about this Bible. Three days before this, I did not have a Bible—but I did have a Bible-believing, tongue-talking mother. The day before this, I received a small package from her but had not opened it. When I received it, I was in a bad mood and just threw the package down the hallway. It slid into the bedroom and went under the bed. Jesus knew this. That was why He could tell me to look under the bed!

I reached under the bed, took out the package, and opened it. Then I said, "Lord, where do I start?" Jesus said, *"Open it and start reading."* Without flipping a page, I opened the Bible and started reading. The first scriptures I read in my life as a Christian were 1 Peter 4:1-11 (at some point, I believe I will write a book that will detail the revelations I have received on these scriptures over the years). *I will tell you this much: every mistake I have made as a Christian has been because I was not living out the truths and details of these verses. When you and I learn to live out 1 Peter 4:1-11, there will be no mistakes!*

Living for God

So then, since Christ suffered physical pain, you must arm yourselves with the same attitude he had, and be ready to suffer, too. For if you are willing to suffer for Christ, you have decided to stop sinning. And you won't spend the rest of your life chasing after evil desires, but you will be anxious to do the will of God. You have had enough in the past of the evil things that godless people enjoy—their immorality and lust, their feasting and drunkenness and wild parties, and their terrible worship of idols. Of course, your former friends are very surprised when you no longer join them in the wicked things they do, and they say evil things about you. But just remember that they will have to face God, who will judge everyone, both the living and the dead. That is why the Good News was preached even to those who have died—so that although their bodies were punished with death, they could still live in the spirit as God does. The end of the world is coming soon. Therefore, be earnest and disciplined in your prayers. Most important of all, continue to show deep love for each other, for love covers a multitude of sins. Cheerfully share your home with those who need a meal or a place to stay. God has given gifts to each of you from his great variety of spiritual gifts. Manage them well so that God's generosity can flow through you. Are you called to be a speaker? Then speak as though God himself were speaking through you. Are you called to help others? Do it with all the strength and energy that God supplies. Then God will be given glory in everything through Jesus Christ. All glory and power belong to him forever and ever. Amen (1 Peter 4:1-11, *NLT*).

These verses were not given to me so that I would become born again. It took me a while to understand this: I was already born again before I read these verses, because the first thing I said to Jesus was, "Lord!" I called Him Lord before I even asked a question. *These verses, as well as all the others, were given as our guideline for life.*

"Follow Me"

He said, *"Follow Me."* Jesus is such a great Teacher. He shows us how to accomplish what He instructs by the Holy Spirit. Then, He lets us practice. He demonstrates to us over and over until we get it. Do you remember when you were in grade school? The teacher taught you to add two plus two by telling you, showing you, and letting you practice over and over until you understood and remembered. Once you learned a lesson, you were promoted.

The Father, Jesus, and the Holy Spirit are better at teaching than the best teacher you ever had in school. They have more patience, and they know infinitely more. They want you to learn so that you can be promoted in the kingdom of God.

Jesus said, *"Follow Me."* Not some man, but Jesus. Yes, we can learn from people who have spent time with Jesus, His Word, and with the Holy Spirit. The Bible says in Ephesians 4:11-13 that such people have gifts from Jesus, given to them to help us grow:

> *And he gave some, apostles; and some, prophets; and some, evangelists; and some, pastors and teachers; For the perfecting of the saints, for the work of the ministry, for the edifying of the body of Christ: Till we all come in the unity of the faith, and of the knowledge of the Son of God, unto a perfect man, unto the measure of the stature of the fullness of Christ.*

Verses 12-13 reveal why Jesus gives these gifts. First Corinthians 12:28 also lists those who are set in the Church to help us: *"...first apostles, secondarily prophets, thirdly teachers, after that miracles, then gifts of healings, helps, governments, diversities of tongues."* We can also learn from each other as believers in the Body of Christ. But, our Chief Teacher must always be Jesus Himself. He said, *"Follow Me."*

"I Have Called You"

Jesus said, *"I have called you."* I believe that *every person has been called*—called to be His child, called to be full of the Spirit, called to follow Him, called to grow up and mature in Him, called to witness, called to be healed, called to be blessed, and called to be a blessing.

Did you ever think about the fact that Jesus Himself, the Son of God, had to spend time on earth growing up and maturing? He began as a baby in Bethlehem, and then He was a child. The Bible says, *"...the child grew, and waxed strong in spirit, filled with wisdom; and the grace of God was upon him"* (Luke 2:40). Why did Jesus need to mature? *So that He would be in the condition and position to fulfill the entire ministry that God had for Him.* He learned to hear and to be attentive to the Father's voice—He learned to obey even unto the very death on the cross that purchased salvation, healing, and deliverance for us (Philippians 2:8).

Romans 11:29 says, *"...the gifts and calling of God are without repentance."* This means that the gifts and callings God gives are eternal. Once God gives them to us, they are ours forever. God won't "change His mind" and take them away from us. But, He leaves the choice up to us, whether or not to use the gifts or to walk in the calling He's bestowed.

Jesus said, *"I have called you."* These words have been very important to me personally and in growing and doing the works of Jesus. I could not have written this book 20 years ago. I have been studying and learning God's Word, by the Holy Spirit and by experience, as I practice over and over what the Lord has shown me to do.

This word *call* is very important—it means, "to make a request or demand, to summon to a particular activity or office." There are many calls. We can get calls from every direction and from all kinds of people. Jesus calls. The Holy Spirit calls. The Devil calls. People call. Our flesh calls. Just think about it—calls, calls, calls, calls, calls, and more calls! I think you get the point. Make sure you understand this: when someone calls you, it puts the responsibility on *you*. It is left up to you to respond, "Yes" or, "No" to the call. How will you respond to the Lord's call on your life?

After you respond, you must also choose your reaction. Will you react to the call with a good attitude or a bad one? For instance, you can be called to wash the dishes and decide to say, "Yes, I'll wash them," yet still rise to the call with a bad attitude. *Your attitude in responding to your calling determines the kind of fruit that calling will produce—and whether or not that fruit will last.*

♦♦♦♦♦♦♦

But ye are a chosen generation, a royal priesthood, an holy nation, a peculiar people; that ye should shew forth the praises of him who hath called you out of darkness into his marvellous light... (1 Peter 2:9).

4

ANOTHER COMFORTER FOR US

There was one last thing that Jesus said to me the night I saw Him face to face. Remember, He said, *"You will not see me anymore like this as long as you live on the face of the earth."* I did not realize the importance of that statement until I received the Baptism in the Holy Spirit several years later. Then I understood what Jesus meant.

In John 16:7, Jesus told the disciples that He was going away. That meant that they would not be able to see Him any more the way they had been seeing Him. He was leaving. His time and work on earth was coming to a close. Jesus said, *"Nevertheless I tell you the truth; It is expedient for you that I go away: for if I go not away, the Comforter will not come unto you; but if I depart, I will send him unto you"* (John 16:7).

God loved the world so much that He gave His only begotten Son (John 3:16). Jesus loved God's children so much that He asked the Father to send the Holy Spirit. *Jesus was the Father's gift of love to the world. The Holy Spirit was His gift of love to His children.*

Here are the Father, Jesus, and the Holy Spirit doing something for our benefit first so that we can be of benefit to someone else. Jesus said, *"It is expedient for you that I go away...."* That simply means that it was for our advantage, for our benefit, that

Jesus went away and sent the Holy Spirit. I don't know about you, but if something is for my advantage, I want it!

You Don't Have to Seek a Vision

I am so glad that Jesus said, *"You will not see me anymore like this as long as you live on the face of the earth."* We don't have to seek a dream or a vision to get directions or to hear His voice: we have the Living Word of God and the Holy Spirit. It is very important that you understand how these two work together to guide you. God's will for your life is found in His Word, the Bible. Be aware, though, that there are some things that are His will for you to do that may not be specifically outlined in His Word—but they always will be supported by the Word.

Let me give you an example. It was God's will for my wife and I to go to the Philippines, but we did not find that specifically in the Bible. You do find, *"Go ye into all the world..."* (Mark 16:15) there, but you won't find, "Go ye, James Rushton, into the Philippines." It will take the voice of the Holy Spirit to direct you to go to a specific location. Be assured that you can trust Him to guide you, because Holy Spirit knows the mind of God (1 Corinthians 2:9-11):

> *But as it is written, Eye hath not seen, nor ear heard, neither have entered into the heart of man, the things which God hath prepared for them that love him. But God hath revealed them unto us by his Spirit: for the Spirit searcheth all things, yea, the deep things of God. For what man knoweth the things of a man, save the spirit of man which is in him? even so the things of God knoweth no man, but the Spirit of God.*

Another Comforter

The Holy Spirit is the Other Comforter that Jesus promised to send: *"And I will pray the Father, and he shall give you another Comforter, that he may abide with you for ever"* (John 14:16). Why did Jesus say that? Was it because He was leaving and wanted to cheer up His disciple? Were those just empty words? Just what did the Father and Jesus have in mind here?

They had in mind for us to do the works of Jesus so that our joy could be full (John 14:12; John 15:11). They knew that for us to be able to do these works, we would need help, counsel, and strength. They knew that we would need someone to stand by us, someone who could be our advocate and intercessor.

What is Another Comforter? *Another* means, "the same kind, but different." Suppose you had a dollar bill and sent it away to someone; then, someone gave you another one. Would you still have the same kind of dollar bill? Yes, but it would be a different one.

Jesus did not say "another savior." He said, *"...another Comforter...."* A *comforter* is, "something or someone that gives aid, relief, or support in times of distress or sorrow." *The Holy Spirit has been sent to bring aid, relief, and support!* Many full-gospel people have missed out on much joy and many blessings, because they put too much emphasis on praying and speaking in tongues and not enough on the *Person* Who *is* the Other Comforter. We need both, but why pray in His language if you do not want to know Him?

Jesus: The First Comforter

Jesus was a Comforter to the disciples and to others as He walked the earth. He comforted them in varying ways. Once, Peter, full of boldness as usual, said to the Lord, *"If that be thou, bid me to come unto thee on the water."* Jesus said, *"Come"* (Matthew 14:28-29). When Jesus says that you can come, you can—as long as you keep your eyes on Him and not on your surroundings. Peter started out just fine until he observed the wind and the waves. That's when he became distressed—he needed help; he needed relief.

Jesus comforted him by stretching out His hand and by catching him as he began to sink. Jesus said, *"O thou of little faith, wherefore didst thou doubt?"* Peter had a little faith, but Peter doubted; yet that didn't stop Jesus from reaching out and helping him. Peter started out with his eyes on Jesus. Then, just to make sure of what he was seeing, he said, "Lord, if it's You, tell me to come." What else was Jesus to do? Jesus told him to come. Why? Because Peter did have his eyes on Jesus at first—and he was seeking truth.

Jesus said, *"...Come..."*—just one word. You do not need to know everything before you can live by faith and get help. You *do* need to keep your eyes on Jesus, and you *do* need to be certain that the words in which you are putting your faith are His.

Second Chronicles 16:9 says, *"For the eyes of the LORD run to and fro throughout the whole earth, to shew himself strong in the behalf of them whose heart is perfect toward him."* Isn't that what happened here? Peter turned his eyes toward the Lord, and Jesus said, *"Come"* so that He could reveal truth to Peter.

Then, Peter took his eyes off Jesus—at that moment, there was no demonstration of the Lord's power. Peter experienced distress. But, when Peter put his eyes back on the Lord, Jesus showed Himself strong. Notice that Peter not only turned his eyes toward Jesus, he *said* something. I have found that when it seems like my life is going up and down like the waves of the sea, I have to stop and refocus my eyes on Jesus and His Word. It is then that I am comforted and find relief. Why is this effective? *When you turn your eyes to the Lord and focus on His Word in faith, it influences the Holy Spirit to perform as He needs to.*

There is another example of Jesus' comforting His disciples in a time of distress in Matthew 8:23-27. They were all in a boat with Jesus when the wind and seas began to stir up. They became so fearful that they began to wonder if Jesus still loved them! They asked Him, *"Master, carest thou not that we perish?"* Of course Jesus cared about them, and He cares for you, too. That's why He asked the Father to send the Holy Spirit. It doesn't matter what kind of storm you are facing. Regardless of the distress, He cares for and wants to comfort and help you just as He did for the disciples. Every time they needed comfort, they got it—but only after they turned their eyes toward Him.

There was another time when over 5,000 people needed comfort. They were hungry and needed relief. Jesus comforted them with fish and bread until all were satisfied (Matthew 14:14-21). He cared for them.

Before He left this earth, Jesus promised the disciples, *"I will not leave you comfortless..."* (John 14:18). As promised, He asked the Father to send another Comforter, the Holy Spirit. Now, when you need relief, the Holy Spirit can take care of you just as Jesus took care of His disciples—if you will ask. He is

35

the one called along side us to comfort us, help us, strengthen us, stand by us, be a Counselor to us, help our prayers of intercession, be our Advocate, teach us, and guide us. Jesus did all of these things for His disciples, and the Holy Spirit will do the same for us. He is Another Comforter—the same kind, but different.

◆◆◆◆◆◆◆

For the eyes of the LORD range throughout the earth to strengthen those whose hearts are fully committed to him (2 Chronicles 16:9, *NIV*).

5

OUR GUARANTEE

The first work of the Holy Spirit in my life was when I was 14 years old. I was asked to read the scriptures at a youth meeting held in the church I attended. I belonged to this church, but I was not born again (my mother was a Christian; but my father was not a believer at this time, although he did become a child of God later in his life).

Our church was one of those old churches where you had to walk up six steps to get to the pulpit. I started up the steps with absolutely no interest in God. I just wanted to read and get out of there! As I took the first three steps, a small bright light started shining right above me, and I heard a voice say, *"This is where you belong."* Although I heard the words very clearly, I did not respond correctly. I just read those scriptures and ran!

It was many years later that I obeyed that voice. I believe the Holy Spirit was telling me that I belonged in the family of God and in the ministry.

Saved for Something

My next experience with the things of God occurred when I was 16 years old. I was in a car with two high-school buddies. We were going to the beach (we were supposed to be in school, but we decided not to go that day). I was not driving; I was in the front passenger seat. We were traveling along at over 100 miles an hour, trying to go around a curve before a drawbridge. It was not just a little curve: the warning sign said 35 miles per hour, but we were going over 100! The driver lost control, so we hit the bridge and another car. It seemed as though we hit everything in sight.

We all ended up in the hospital. Although I had no broken bones, I had a concussion and was in a coma for many days. The morning I regained consciousness, an old lady came into the room. This was no ordinary lady. She was a Spirit-filled Christian. Keep in mind, this happened back in 1957—there weren't too many of them around back then!

She walked into the room like she owned it. She was only about five feet tall, but she was ten feet tall with the Holy Ghost. This woman knew me: she was my great aunt. She raised my mother, because my mother's mother died when my mother was only six years old. My great aunt raised my mother and five other children with no husband (he had died) and no help from the government.

She walked up to the bed, put her hand on my forehead, looked me straight in the eyes, and said, "Jimmy, Jesus loves you, and He saved you for something." I've already shared with you about my face-to-face encounter with Jesus that happened on a November night in 1969. The first words Jesus told me that night had a familiar ring: "Jimmy, I love you and I saved you for something." Over the years, I've seen these words come to pass.

You see, when the Holy Spirit—or anyone led by the Spirit—tells you something, you can rest assured that the Holy Spirit can back it up 100 percent. When people respond correctly, He backs them up. He backs up everything the Father ever said; He backs up everything Jesus said; and He backs up every word of the Bible. When someone believes by saying what He wants said, He backs it up!

It's Guaranteed!

The Holy Spirit is the down payment, or the guarantee, that we will receive whatever God has said to us by His Word and by His Spirit. Everything God promises to us about our new life in Christ is guaranteed from start to finish—when we believe. Second Corinthians 1:22 (*NLT*) makes this clear: *"...and he has identified us as his own by placing the Holy Spirit in our hearts as the first installment of everything he will give us."*

Ephesians 1:13-14 (*NKJV*) states, *"In Him* [Jesus] *you also trusted, after you heard the word of truth, the gospel of your salvation, in whom also, having believed, you were sealed with the Holy Spirit of promise, who is the guarantee of our inheritance."* The guarantee is two-fold:

1. When we call on the name of the Lord for salvation, we receive eternal life.
2. When we believe and confess, we receive the desires of our heart based on His Word.

It's interesting how Jesus and the Holy Spirit work together to bring us eternal life. Jesus paid the price—He paid for our salvation and all God has for us. Then, the Holy Spirit convinces us that we need to call on the name of the Lord to be saved. Men may be used to share the gospel with you, but it takes the Holy Spirit to convince you and show you the truth—and then back that truth up when you believe.

Today, when we buy a house, we put up a deposit, called earnest money. It assures the seller of the house that we are sincere and that more money will follow. In the same way, *God gives the Holy Spirit to us in advance as a pledge that more will follow.* Having the Holy Spirit already in our hearts as a down payment helps us to walk by faith in the promises of God.

> *For all the promises of God in Him are Yes, and in Him Amen, to the glory of God by us. Now He who establishes us with you in Christ and has anointed us is God, who also has sealed us and given us the Spirit in our hearts as a deposit* (2 Corinthians 1:20-22, *NKJV*).

> *Now He who has prepared us for this very thing is God, who also has given us the Spirit as a deposit* (2 Corinthians 5:5, *NKJV*).

What Did God Say?

In Luke 1:26-37, when the angel, Gabriel, told Mary that she was going to have a child, the angel was sent by God. Gabriel said what God wanted said, to whom God wanted it said, the way God wanted it said, and when God wanted it said.

Mary's response was, "How can this be?"

The angel said, "By the Holy Spirit."

The Holy Spirit is the one who guarantees what God has said when we say, "Let it be according to Thy Word."

When you need healing in your body, it is also the Holy Spirit who guarantees that you will receive that healing—when you believe God's Word in your heart and confess what you believe with your mouth. You may be thinking, "Wait a minute! Jesus is my healer. You are leaving out Jesus." No, Jesus is still very much involved.

Jesus is the One that made all that we need. The Holy Spirit just delivers what we believe. Jesus and the Word of God are one and the same (John 1:1-14). When we believe and speak God's Word, the Holy Spirit will guarantee it to come to pass just as it was spoken. If it is spoken the way God said, when God said, to whom or what God said, and is believed, the Holy Spirit will deliver.

Included in the Purchase Price

When you go to a store and buy an appliance, you pay for it out of your own pocket. Then, the store's owner tells you that it is yours. He guarantees that it will work properly for three years. Who paid for the guarantee? You did! It was added into the total price before the appliance was ever put in the store.

That is what the Godhead—the Father, Jesus and the Holy Spirit—did with the guarantee of our salvation. He added it to the purchase price. The Persons of the Godhead planned and created the world and all that is in it. Then they made man in their own image and gave the man, Adam, the responsibility of overseeing what they had made. But something happened: Adam and his wife sinned. They went the way of the flesh, right into the trap of the Devil; in so doing, they lost it all. They sold out to the Devil and let him have the earth.

So the Father had a "board meeting" in heaven with Jesus and the Holy Spirit and said, "We are going to get this planet back. But, it is going to cost, and we will have to guarantee the results."

Jesus said, "What will it cost?'

The Father said, "Your life. But, don't worry—the Holy Spirit will guarantee you your life back. Everything will work out as planned as long as you operate according to the Owner's Manual."

Jesus paid the price and operated His life according to that Owner's Manual—the Word of God. Jesus belonged, and still does, to God. He did not sell out. You (if you are born again) and I belong to God as well. Jesus purchased back everything Adam gave to the Devil. Jesus put it back in His storehouse for us so that we can receive it all by faith. All we need to do is fulfill our part of the contract. The Holy Spirit guarantees what belongs to us will be ours when we believe correctly.

How do we know this? Because God wrote the contract and made the guarantee. The Father wrote the policy, Jesus did His part and signed it in His blood, and the Holy Spirit sealed it with His guarantee. God gave it all to us. He gave us what He purchased, giving us a copy of the agreement, the bill of sale, and our certificate of guarantee. We know, because we chose to believe God and His Word. Let us operate by the Owner's Manual that He gave us.

God's Word says, *"For whosoever shall call upon the name of the Lord shall be saved"* (Romans 10:13). These words were paid for by Jesus, and the Holy Spirit guarantees that they will come to pass. This is true with every promise in the Bible.

So Why Isn't it Working for Me?

You might ask, "If all of the promises are guaranteed like you say, why don't I see them working in my life?". Think of it this way: suppose you buy a car. The sellers tell you that the engine is guaranteed for 100,000 miles, but the fine print in the owner's manual says that you must change the oil at certain times and use a certain type of oil. Additionally, you must use a certain type of water, treated with the correct amount of anti-freeze, and keep it at the right level. All of these conditions must be met for the guarantee to be in effect.

Why must you use oil and water? So that the engine will continue running smoothly and remain cool. This is why we need the oil of the Spirit and the water of the Word—so that we will keep running smoothly and remain cool. No water? You loose your cool. No oil? You sound like an engine knocking. Get low on either one of these two, and you'll get hot and explode.

Regardless, you never read the owner's manual. You just drive and drive and drive. You never change the oil or check the water level. You don't even raise the hood to check anything! You just drive and drive and drive. Then one day, the engine goes, "Kalunk-kalunk." You take your car to the dealership and demand that they fix it, saying, "It's guaranteed!"

"First," they say, "let us check something." They do some checking and discover that you never changed the oil. Not only that, you did not even check it. You didn't keep the oil at its proper level. The engine blew up, because you did not carry out your part of the contract. And the bottom line? You find out that the guarantee is void because of your neglect.

The way you take care of yourself has an effect on others and how they are blessed. Why? If you are not operating in the Spirit with the Word of God, you will have a negative effect on those around you.

You need to take the time to read the "fine print" of your contract—the Bible. Maybe you are full of knowledge about the promises; but, you still need to read the "fine print" of any conditions that must be met so that the guarantee will remain in effect. You may find that you need to raise your water level in the Word and your oil level in the Spirit!

The Word of God is the water for your spirit man. Jesus said to Nicodemus, *"Verily, verily, I say unto thee, Except a man be born of water and of the Spirit, he cannot enter into the kingdom of God"* (John 3:7). Not only are you to be born of the water, but you are to take in water (the Word) every day. Water is something you need every day. Your natural body needs water to live. Why? It keeps your body cool and keeps your system clean. Ephesians 5:26 says, *"That he might sanctify and cleanse it with the washing of water by the word...."*

While we are on the subject of cleansing, there is another thing you need to have active in your life, and that is the blood of Jesus. The Word cleans your mind; the blood cleans you of all sin. The following passages make this clear:

> *For this is my blood of the new testament, which is shed for many for the remission of sins* (Matthew 26:28).

> *Whom God hath set forth to be a propitiation through faith in his blood, to declare his righteousness for the remission of sins that are past, through the forbearance of God...* (Romans 3:25).

In whom we have redemption through his blood, the forgiveness of sins, according to the riches of his grace (Ephesians 1:7).

And almost all things are by the law purged with blood; and without shedding of blood is no remission (Hebrews 9:2).

But if we walk in the light, as he is in the light, we have fellowship one with another, and the blood of Jesus Christ his Son cleanseth us from all sin (1 John 1:7).

Your spirit man also needs the oil of the Spirit. Throughout the Scriptures oil is use as a type of the Spirit. The following scriptures illustrate further:

Thou hast loved righteousness, and hated iniquity; therefore God, even thy God, hath anointed thee with the oil of gladness above thy fellows (Hebrews 1:9).

Thou preparest a table before me in the presence of mine enemies: thou anointest my head with oil; my cup runneth over (Psalm 23:5).

Take Care of What's Inside

Remember, it's not the outside of the automobile that keeps it going. It's what's on the inside—what's under the hood and how it is taken care of and driven—that makes it run smoothly and last many miles. The same is true for you. *Whatever is inside of you determines your destiny.*

Do you want your faith, your love, your prosperity, your healing, your preaching, your teaching, and all other things available to you from God to be backed up, sealed, and guaranteed by the Holy Spirit? Then stay clean, stay pure, and stay in right standing with God and with those with whom you live and work. Live peaceably with all men by keeping your water (Word) and oil (Spirit) levels up. This equates not just to having *feelings* of love, but true compassion.

Jesus taught the Sermon on the Mount so that we would know how to live in such a way that we would be supported and backed up by the Holy Spirit. All God's promises require support through proper care within our hearts for the guarantee to be activated. Just like the car, we must tend properly to ourselves *inside* for the guarantee to apply.

That is why God gave to the Body of Christ apostles, prophets, evangelists, pastors, and teachers—to help us to remain fine-tuned so that the guarantee would stay in effect. He wants us all to come into unity of the faith, to know Jesus, and to measure up to the stature of the fullness of Christ. He doesn't want us to be tossed around by the empty winds of false doctrines (Ephesians 4:11-16).

Why is the guarantee of the Holy Spirit so important? God wants us to be able to effectively do the works of the ministry. How can we do the works of Jesus if we don't have the Holy Spirit backing us up? And, how can the Holy Spirit back up what we say and do unless we are attuned with God, saying what He wants said, to whom He wants it said, when He wants it said, and how He wants it said?

Praise God for the Owners Manual, His written Word. It is for our use to get our minds renewed—not just to know what is ours, but also to learn what we should do to keep our guarantee activated. Praise God that we have the blood of Jesus that cleanses our spirit and the oil of the Spirit to keep us running "clean and smooth." When you are clean, you can breathe in and breathe out the things of God.

Praise God that we have one another in Christ so that we may help each other learn to walk in the love of God and grow in Christ. Praise God that we have the Holy Spirit to back us up as we do the works of Jesus. And, praise God that He came to teach us and lead on the right path so that He can back us up.

♦♦♦♦♦♦♦

Thus saith the LORD, thy Redeemer, the Holy One of Israel; I am the LORD thy God which teacheth thee to profit, which leadeth thee by the way that thou shouldest go (Isaiah 48:17).

Another...: The Same Kind, but Different

6

OUR COUNSELOR AND ADVOCATE

Before He left the earth, Jesus said, *"And I will pray the Father, and he shall give you another Comforter,* [Counselor, Helper, Intercessor, Advocate, Strengthener, and Standby] *that he may abide with you for ever"* (John 14:16).

As we look at each of these more closely, I want to encourage you to have faith in what Jesus promised the Other Comforter would do to and for us. Remember, *"Without faith it is impossible to please God for he that cometh to God must believe that He is and that He is a rewarder of those who diligently seek Him"* (Hebrews 11:6).

Faith is "a firm belief or confidence in the honesty, integrity, reliability, and justice of another person or thing." *Faith involves your putting your trust, confidence, and dependence in another person's words, actions, judgment, character, and attitude.* We need to have and release this kind of faith in God the Father, in Jesus, in the Holy Spirit, and in their words. We need to believe that what Jesus said about the Holy Spirit is true. In our relationship with the Holy Spirit, let's have faith in Him as another Comforter and as our Counselor, Helper, Intercessor, Advocate, Strengthener, and Standby.

Our Counselor

A *counselor* is "someone who gives legal advice, but does not make the decision." One of the functions of the Holy Spirit is to be, *"...the spirit of counsel..."* (Isaiah 11:2).

If you go to a lawyer for counsel, he will give you legal advice—but *you* have to make the decision as to which action you will take. *It is the same with the Holy Spirit. He will give us true counsel, but we must make the decisions as to what to do.* If you want counsel that will influence you to make the *right* decisions, you must be honest and go to a counselor who is honest and in touch with God and His Word.

The Holy Spirit's counsel comes from two sources: the written Word of God and from God directly, because He knows the mind of God. It takes the Holy Spirit to tell us how to carry out God's Word and His directions.

How many times have we been guilty of making bad decisions, because we would not take heed to what the Spirit was saying? How many times has someone not been blessed because of our not listening to His counsel? So many times we let our heads and fleshly feelings get in the way.

Many times, the best bits of counsel the Holy Spirit will give you will come in a form of questions. I have not always picked up on this like I should have. But, Praise God, I have learned. One of the most frequent questions the Holy Spirit has used in counseling me is, *"Can you afford it?"* For example, can you afford that house or car? Can you afford to spend time with that person or persons? Can you afford not to study the Word? Can you afford not to walk in love? Can you afford not to forgive? Can you afford not to pray? Can you afford not to give tithes and offerings?

When I first stepped out in obedience to go to Bible school, I saw God do some great things for me. I obeyed Him with all the faith I had. One instance was when I started to go from South Carolina to Oklahoma to go to school, driving a Chevrolet Blazer. When I arrived in Tennessee, the engine blew up. I had it hauled to a Chevrolet dealership and told them my story. Then the salesman asked me a question: "Do you have good credit?" I said, "Yes." He checked me out—and I drove away from the dealership in a brand new little car. This was great for me at the time, because it fit my budget.

The rest of this story took place while I was attending RHEMA Bible Training Center (RHEMA). I worked for RHEMA and spent all of my free time praying and studying. But, one day, I just became tired of praying and studying and decided to go look at cars. I went directly to the Chevy place. Then I saw it—I saw the Monte Carlo that was for me. It was my color, my style. So, I stopped to take a closer look. The more I looked, the more it was "mine." Then the salesman came up and started showing me all the extras it had. Then I said (without praying, without asking the Holy Spirit), "What will you give me for my car, and how much will the payments be?" He answered me, and I said, "Okay."

Then I drove off with my car, the one *I* had to have. Not once did I ask myself, "Can you afford this?" Not once did I ask the Holy Spirit for counsel about the purchase. Not once did the salesman ask me the question, "Can you afford it?" I have never seen a sales person ask that question. All they want to know is if you want it and if you have good credit or cash. There is a difference between being able to afford to buy something and having good credit. *Just because you have good credit, it does not mean you can afford it.* I wonder how many new homes and cars would be sold if they asked the question, "Can you afford to buy this?"

I am not proud of that example, but I pray that you get the message from it and that you let it be a piece of counsel from the Lord for you. Can you afford it? Have you counted the cost? This question is to be asked of everything. Can you afford to change jobs? Can you afford to go to the church you go to? What is one of the things you can look at to see if you can afford it? Judge it by its fruit, by the fruit it is producing or will produce.

We need to count the cost in every area of our lives, not just with money matters. Many times we need direction in how to truly love someone or advice on how to reconcile a relationship. Some times we've offended people and didn't even know we did. When you know something has taken place that offended someone, you need to pray and ask the Holy Spirit what to do. He may give you the counsel to do nothing but walk in love and act as though it never happened.

And, why might it be appropriate to act as though nothing ever happened? Because many times what some people would call an offense is not really an offense; rather, it may well be that the person who seemed to be offended was just in a bad mood. In this kind of situation, it might be better to not push the issue, but to walk in love with the person and ask the Holy Spirit to help encourage the person, influencing him or her into the mood of Christ—the joy of the Lord.

Then there are times when the Holy Spirit may tell you to go talk with the person in private and to get it cleared up. Most of the time, it is some little thing—and when it is over, you just laugh together over it. It doesn't take long to get over it if you do your part under the direction of the Holy Spirit.

Advocate

As we look at these words about the Other Comforter separately, it does not mean that they operate separately. Just like the word *counselor*—it flows right along with the word *advocate*, but an advocate does more than just give counsel.

When you have an Advocate, not only will you receive advice—your Advocate will plead your case in your favor! In today's language, we might use the word *lawyer* or *attorney* instead of the word *advocate*.

There have been many times in my "B.C." days (before Christ) when I needed a lawyer. I remember the first time very well. I was only 14 years of age. In those days, you could get your driver's license at the age of 14, and that is what I did on my fourteenth birthday. Two weeks later, I needed a lawyer. My father got the family lawyer to take my case. He was a big man, about six feet and six inches tall—and to me, he looked to be 80 years old.

Other than not paying a fine, this is what I remember about this incident. When I walked into the lawyer's office, the first thing he said was, "Jimmy, do not say one word. Let me do all the talking for you." Now, with this lawyer, he *did* do all the talking. How does this work with the Holy Spirit as our Advocate? The main difference is who is doing the talking. In my case in court on earth, it was the lawyer my father had hired that did all the talking. He was even coming up with the words.

When you allow the Holy Spirit to be your Advocate in a time of need or trouble, He will come up with the words that need to be spoken—just like my lawyer did in court. Here is the difference: in court, a man spoke for me. *The Holy Spirit cannot do your talking—you must actually use your mouth to form the words—*

but the Holy Spirit will give you the words to speak. Not only will He give you the words, but He will also tell you how to speak them and when. But, He can only do this completely when you totally let Him be your Lawyer, without your "butting in" and trying to run the show.

See it! You allow Him to be your Advocate, but He lets you be the mouthpiece. As Jesus allowed the Holy Spirit to be His Advocate, the Holy Spirit did the same thing for Jesus. The Holy Spirit always gave Jesus the words to speak but did not do the talking. There were even a few times when the Holy Spirit, as Jesus' Advocate, told Jesus just to be quiet.

Remember, this takes faith. To have faith in the Other Comforter as your Advocate, you will have to trust His judgment, His words, and His actions—and flow with them. He has given you everything pertaining to life and godliness. It is yours if you will only listen and act on the instructions your Counselor and Advocate gives you. Yes, we all miss it sometimes by not yielding to Him; but remember, His mercies are new each morning, and we can ask for forgiveness. In Isaiah 11:1-3 there is a prophecy about Jesus:

> *And there shall come forth a rod out of the stem of Jesse, and a Branch shall grow out of his roots: And the spirit of the Lord shall rest upon him, the spirit of wisdom and understanding, the spirit of counsel and might, the spirit of knowledge and of the fear of the Lord: And shall make him of quick understanding in the fear of the Lord: and he shall not judge after the sight of his eyes, neither reprove after the hearing of his ears...*

These same spirits that were available in and for Jesus are available in and for you. Let us draw from them. Let us use them. Let us allow the Holy Spirit to work all the way in each and every way. Jesus needed Him and allowed the Holy Spirit to work in Him, for Him, and through Him. Jesus knew the Holy Spirit was with Him.

♦♦♦♦♦♦♦

You are of God, little children, and have overcome them, because He who is in you is greater than he who is in the world (1 John 4:4, *NKJV*).

7

OUR HELPER

" I have a job to do, and I would appreciate your allowing me to do it." He went on to say, *"My job is to do for you what I did for God and Jesus. I helped God make and create the earth and man. I helped Jesus be like the Father and do the works the Father wanted Him to do. They needed and use me, so why don't you?"* These words were given to me when I was going through a hard time and was depending on man, the arm of the flesh, more than I was depending on the Holy Spirit. During this time, I did turn my eyes toward Him. He spoke further to me, saying, *"By definition, a helper makes it easier for something to happen or exist: he shares the labor, but does not do it all."*

We are looking at these attributes separately to get a better understanding of each one other than just *Comforter.* But, keep in mind that these functions of the Holy Spirit do not work independently. When one works, there is another one working also in complete support of the first. For example, if He is operating as a Strengthener, He is also helping. If He is your Advocate, He is also giving counsel, etc.

The Holy Spirit wants to help us be like Christ and do like Christ. But, for Him to be our Helper, we must let Him help us and allow Him to do it His way. He will bring us into maturity in Christ Jesus if we will only listen and obey. *We need to actively believe that He will help us live the Christian life.* If we want His full help, we must put faith in how He wants to help us and flow with Him. Jesus said in Matthew 11:28-30:

> *Come unto me, all ye that labour and are heavy laden, and I will give you rest. Take my yoke upon you, and learn of me; for I am meek and lowly in heart: and ye shall find rest unto your souls. For my yoke is easy, and my burden is light.*

I think the disciples had an easier time understanding this than we do. Jesus was standing right there with them, helping them do all things. We don't have Jesus with us just exactly the way they did. But, we do have His Word, and we have the Holy Spirit in us.

When Jesus spoke these words, He meant that, after we put on His yoke, we should *stay* hooked up with Him and His Word, and let the Holy Spirit help us learn of Him and His ways. He meant for us to stay hooked up—until it is finished. When you allow the Holy Spirit to help you, let Him help you *all the way* until something happens or until something comes into existence.

We are talking about the Holy Spirit's helping us. When you help someone, it does not mean that you do everything for him or her. It means that the other person continues to do his/her part and that you just join in to help finish the job. Just because the burden becomes light does not mean you can quit. Stay on the job until it is finished.

He Wants to Help in All Things

Many times when we read and study about the help of the Holy Spirit, we focus on His help with our prayers. This is based on Romans 8:26 that says, *"Likewise the Spirit also helpeth our infirmities: for we know not what we should pray for as we ought: but the Spirit itself maketh intercession for us with groanings which cannot be uttered."*

The Holy Spirit certainly helps us in prayer, but that is not the only area in which He desires to help. I am not just talking about when we are in trouble. In Psalm 91:15 He promises, *"...I will be with him in trouble..."*; but, as was mentioned before, *if we would allow Him to help on a regular basis, there wouldn't be so much trouble!* There will always be some type of situation in which we will need His help, but let's allow the Holy Spirit free rein in our lives as Helper, and He will help us pass the test. There are many areas in which we never think to ask the Holy Spirit for help. Yet, He desires to help us in all things. Begin today to let the Holy Spirit help you:

1. With worship

   "God is a Spirit: and they that worship him must worship him in spirit and in truth" (John 4:24).

2. With singing

   "...I will sing with the spirit, and I will sing with the understanding also" (1 Corinthians 14:15b).

3. With praying

   "I will pray with the spirit, and I will pray with the understanding also..." (1 Corinthians 14:15a).

"Likewise the Spirit also helpeth our infirmities: for we know not what we should pray for as we ought: but the Spirit itself maketh intercession for us with groanings which cannot be uttered" (Romans 8:26).

4. When you are weak

"He that speaketh in an unknown tongue edifieth himself..." (1 Corinthians 14:4a)

"...building up yourselves on your most holy faith, praying in the Holy Ghost..." (Jude 1:20).

"Likewise the Spirit also helpeth our infirmities..." (Romans 8:26).

5. With witnessing

"And how is it that we hear, each in our own language in which we were born? Cretans and Arabs—we hear them speaking in our own tongues the wonderful works of God" (Acts 2:8,11, *NKJV*).

6. When standing in faith and love

"...building up yourselves on your most holy faith, praying in the Holy Ghost..." (Jude 1:20).

"But the fruit of the Spirit is love, joy, peace, longsuffering, gentleness, goodness, faith, Meekness, temperance: against such there is no law" (Galatians 5:22-23).

Faith alone is dead—there must be corresponding action with what we say in what we do. It takes both confession and action.

Love alone is dead—you can't just *say* you love your wife and accurately call it love. There must be some corresponding action. You cannot just get by with words only. It takes action also.

Forgiveness alone is dead—there must be repentance, or the sin will be committed again. There must be a cleansing, or we will be weighed down. Even if we love God and love one another, for that love to produce we must *act* like it, not just with our words, but also in our deeds.

Don't do like I have done in the past: I would say I loved someone, but then I'd hide whenever I'd see the person coming! Now, I don't do that. Stand with the Word of God and the Spirit of God when reaching out to others, not just talking love but also doing it. That is when it produces.

The Holy Spirit will help you. Let Him help you all the way.

Help in Witnessing

Another reason that Jesus asked the Father to send us the Holy Spirit was to help us to be witnesses*: "But ye shall receive power, after that the Holy Ghost is come upon you: and ye shall be witnesses unto me both in Jerusalem, and in all Judea, and in Samaria, and unto the uttermost part of the earth"* (Acts 1:8).

In Luke 24:46-49, Jesus told His disciples, *"And said unto them, Thus it is written, and thus it behoved Christ to suffer, and to rise from the dead the third day: And that repentance and remission of sins should be preached in his name among all nations, beginning at Jerusalem. And ye are witnesses of these things. And, behold, I send the promise of my Father upon you:*

but tarry ye in the city of Jerusalem, until ye be endued with power from on high."

In John 20:21-22, Jesus said to them again, *"Peace be unto you; as my Father hath sent me, even so send I you. And when he had said this, he breathed on them, and saith unto them, Receive ye the Holy Ghost...."* The Holy Spirit also empowers us to fulfill the Great Commission listed in Mark 16:14-18:

> *Afterward he appeared unto the eleven as they sat at meat, and upbraided them with their unbelief and hardness of heart, because they believed not them which had seen him after he was risen. And he said unto them, Go ye into all the world, and preach the gospel to every creature. He that believeth and is baptized shall be saved; but he that believeth not shall be damned. And these signs shall follow them that believe; In my name shall they cast out devils; they shall speak with new tongues; they shall take up serpents; and if they drink any deadly thing, it shall not hurt them; they shall lay hands on the sick, and they shall recover.*

But wait—don't forget verse 20! If you do not expect this to happen, it won't. Verse 20 says, *"And they went forth, and preached everywhere, the Lord working with them, and confirming the word with signs following."* Amen! So many times we major on Mark 16:14-18 as if it were the only commission. This is just part of it. Let me show you what the other Gospels say with regard to our commission:

> *And Jesus came and spake unto them, saying, All power is given unto me in heaven and in earth. Go ye therefore, and teach all nations, baptizing them in the name of the Father, and of the Son, and of the Holy Ghost: Teaching them to observe all things whatsoever I*

have commanded you: and, lo, I am with you alway, even unto the end of the world. Amen (Matthew 28:18-20).

Then opened he their understanding, that they might understand the scriptures, And said unto them, Thus it is written, and thus it behoved Christ to suffer, and to rise from the dead the third day: And that repentance and remission of sins should be preached in his name among all nations, beginning at Jerusalem. And ye are witnesses of these things (Luke 24:45-48).

Then said Jesus to them again, Peace be unto you: as my Father hath sent me, even so send I you. And when he had said this, he breathed on them, and saith unto them, Receive ye the Holy Ghost: Whosesoever sins ye remit, they are remitted unto them; and whosesoever sins ye retain, they are retained (John 20:21-23).

Have you ever noticed that no one seems to believe a doctrine until they see or hear something? What they see does not have to be a healing or deliverance. It could be forgiveness and reconciliation.

Jesus wants the Holy Spirit to move in us and through us so that there will be signs and wonders manifest. This makes sure that He will be lifted up and draw men unto Him. There can be no signs and wonders to lift up Jesus if the Holy Spirit does not move. Regardless of who is speaking—whether it is God, Jesus, angels, or men—the Holy Spirit must be involved before anything will happen. He is the Helper.

◆ ◆ ◆ ◆ ◆ ◆ ◆

"... Not by might, nor by power, but by my spirit, saith the LORD of hosts" (Zechariah 4:6).

8

OUR STAND-BY AND STRENGTHENER

When I think of the Holy Spirit as my Standby and Strengthener, many examples come to my attention. I recall His standing by me and strengthening me to love and to forgive. I also remember His standing by me and strengthening me to lay hands on the sick and to cast out devils. I think of His standing by me to teach and preach when I did not feel like it— like when a witch doctor was sitting on the front row, and the first thing she said was, "I am going to kill you."

I could write the whole long story of this woman and how my wife and I stood our ground, God using us for her and her family to become born again. We saw the Holy Spirit manifest Himself over and over again. Not just in standing by and strengthening us, we saw miracles, words of wisdom, words of knowledge, and discerning of spirits as we reached this family for Jesus Christ.

Let's read again the Holy Spirit's job description as given by Jesus in John 14:16 (*AMP*): *"And I will ask the Father, and He will give you another Comforter (Counselor, Helper, Intercessor, Advocate, Strengthener, and Standby), that He may remain with you forever...."* This verse not only tells us that the Holy Spirit is Another Comforter, but also that He is Another Counselor, Another Helper, Another Intercessor, Another

Advocate, Another Strengthener, and Another Standby Who will remain with us forever.

Jesus was all of these things to the disciples when He walked on the earth with them. Yet, we can see as we read the gospels that not all of the disciples allowed Him to comfort, counsel, help, stand by, strengthen, or intercede for them or to be their Advocate. Maybe I should say it this way: Jesus made Himself available to do and be all these things and much more for those disciples—just as through His death, burial, and resurrection He made eternal life available to all mankind. But, not all men have received His eternal life, and not all men today allow the Holy Spirit to do His job for them and through them.

Jesus asked the Father to send the Comforter, the Holy Spirit, to all in the Body of Christ, but not all draw from the Comforter. In fact most of the Body of Christ are totally ignorant that their Comforter is the Holy Spirit. They go to men more than they ever go to God. Yes, we are to comfort one another; but, for it to have a lasting effect, it must be under the influence of the Word of God by the direction of the Holy Spirit. Even though we are to comfort one another, man cannot comfort man completely by himself. The Word and the Holy Spirit must be involved. Why? One reason is that no man knows another man's heart completely—but the Holy Spirit does.

The Comforter Knows Your Heart

The prophet tells us in Jeremiah 17:9, *"The heart is deceitful above all things, and desperately wicked: who can know it?"* Men do not know you completely, but the Holy Spirit does. Many times when people go to others for comfort, counsel, help, strength, prayer, or an advocate, they do not share the complete truth. They only disclose what they want them to know. But, it is not this way with the Holy Spirit, for He knows the heart.

You may say, "If He knows? Why doesn't He help?" It could be just because you did not ask. Or, if you did ask, you didn't like His answer or would not wait on it and went on your own way. James 4:2-3 tells us, *"...yet ye have not, because ye ask not. Ye ask, and receive not, because ye ask amiss, that ye may consume it upon your lusts."*

Many times, students and others who worked for us would do things wrong and then come talk to me. Some of the things they did were just mistakes; other things were just plain sin. Many times, one of the last things they would say was, "God knows my heart," indicating that their hearts were right. This could be true if what they did were mere mistakes. But, where there is sin, the heart is not right—and God knows it. The Holy Spirit knows when our hearts are right or wrong. *If you want honest-to-goodness comfort or help, you will have to be completely honest.*

Your Standby

Allow the Holy Spirit to stand by you always. A *standby* is "someone who is always available in time of need and is ready to act as needed on your behalf." Please remember that the Holy Spirit *will* stand by you and is *always* available and ready to act. But if you are not honest and living right, He will be standing by you and telling you to repent and get your act right! He would rather stand by you when you are walking in love and living by faith so that He can stand by you for your victory to manifest.

The Holy Spirit as your Standby is always ready and available to help in a time of need. You may say, "That sounds great, but if He is always ready and available, why is it that I do not get much help?" I'll tell you why. There have been times in my life that He didn't act as needed in the situations I was in. He didn't act, because I didn't put myself in a position *for* Him to act. Do you know what I would do so that He would see no need to act on my behalf? I would put on my "faith face" and act like everything was okay. I would ignore things and go on my merry way. I did not approach Him in faith and ask for His help.

Remember the definition of faith we studied in another chapter? *Faith* is "a firm belief or confidence in the honesty, integrity, reliability, and justice of another person or thing." Faith involves your putting your trust, confidence, and dependence in another person's words, actions, judgment, character, and attitude. *You cannot walk in the true God-kind of faith without having faith in the Holy Spirit—personally putting your faith in Him with your life.*

How do you know that the Holy Spirit is standing by to help in a time of need? Because the Word of God says so. Jesus Himself said in John 14:16-18:

> *And I will pray the Father, and he shall give you another Comforter, that he may abide with you for ever; Even the Spirit of truth; whom the world cannot receive, because it seeth him not, neither knoweth him: but ye know him; for he dwelleth with you, and shall be in you. I will not leave you comfortless: I will come to you.*

You can also know, because you can receive the Baptism in the Holy Spirit with the evidence of speaking in tongues, even if you haven't already. When we pray in the Spirit (in tongues), many things can take place. The more aware you are of someone's presence, the more likely you are to do what would please him or her.

Please don't become so governed by your own needs and desires that you overlook the One standing there, ever ready to help you. Your flesh does not want to help, it just wants its way. The Devil wants to help, but he wants to help you fail. What I want to bring to your attention are some scriptures that support the truth of your being more aware of the Holy Spirit's presence as He stands by you.

But ye, beloved, building up yourselves on your most holy faith, praying in the Holy Ghost, 24 Now unto him that is able to keep you from falling, and to present you faultless before the presence of his glory with exceeding joy (Jude 1:20, 24).

He that speaketh in an unknown tongue edifieth himself; but he that prophesieth edifieth the church (1 Corinthians 14:4).

Likewise the Spirit also helpeth our infirmities: for we know not what we should pray for as we ought: but the Spirit itself maketh intercession for us with groanings which cannot be uttered (Romans 8:26).

Paul, in writing to Timothy in 2 Timothy 1:6-7, said, *"Wherefore I put thee in remembrance that thou stir up the gift of God, which is in thee by the putting on of my hands. For God hath not given us the spirit of fear; but of power, and of love, and of a sound mind."* It is my belief that Paul was talking about the Baptism in the Holy Spirit. Verse seven talks about not having the spirit of fear. *When you are aware of the Holy Spirit's standing by you, there is no need for fear!* When we have no fear, it helps us release the power of love, which helps us to have a sound mind.

In this chapter we are looking at the Holy Spirit as someone like Jesus, as our Standby and Strengthener. But remember that when He is doing these things, other attributes start manifesting, such as the spirit of might, the spirit of wisdom, the spirit of knowledge, and the spirit of understanding (Isaiah 2:11). He wants to stand by and strengthen us to help in every area, not just in the physical realm, but also in our minds and emotions.

Please know and understand that the Holy Spirit is standing by you, but you are the one that causes Him to do more than just stand. When you ask Him, He is standing there waiting for you to initiate so that He can move. He will move if you do your part under His direction.

Strengthener

As Another Comforter, the Holy Spirit is also our Strengthener. To *strengthen* someone is "to make them strong or to help them resist the attack and over come."

Yes, He gives us strength to stand. But He desires to help us to do more than just stand—*He wants to help us to overcome.* Most people have the impression that all Christians do is stand and resist. We are to resist, but to resist does not mean you just stand and "hold the fort." Although there is protection, shelter, and food, there is not much freedom in a fort. Holding the fort is not the same as possessing the land, and that's what the Holy Spirit has come to empower us to do.

When I was in the U.S. Army, I was stationed at an army fort. There was protection, shelter, food, and even fellowship, but we were restricted to a certain area. In order for us to overtake the enemy and have freedom to possess the land, we had to venture out beyond the fort.

In the early days in the development of this country, the people many times just held the fort. But, praise the Lord, they didn't stay in the fort! No, they got out and possessed and developed the land. Can you imagine what it would be like today if all they did was hold down the fort?

Think about King Saul and his army of men in 1 Samuel 17. They were standing fast, or "holding the fort." They were being clothed, fed, and had fellowship, but they were not free. There is no freedom in merely standing your ground.

Then comes this little shepherd boy, David. David was a free man. Sure, he had held his ground, or "fort," before as a shepherd for the protection of the sheep when the bear and the lion came. But, he didn't just stand there! No, he stood and moved in the strength of the Lord. Because of his obedience to do more than stand, the sheep were set free to enjoy the land where they belonged. God did not make you to be trapped in a fort all your life. He created you to be free to possess the land that He's given you.

So, here came David to where King Saul and his army had been standing their ground. Then, do you know what David did? He went on the offense—he got out of the fort and destroyed their enemy; he went forth in the power of the Lord to face and slay Goliath. *You cannot destroy your enemy by simply "holding the fort"—that's just resisting.* And there's no rest in resisting—it's a constant struggle that can wear you down. But God intends for us to be free in Jesus Christ. We are to allow the Holy Spirit to not only stand by us, but also to give us the strength to start advancing to overcome the Enemy and to take possession of the ground God has already given to us.

Yes, there are times you do need to stand and hold the fort, but just hold it long enough to get the wisdom and strength of God to move forward. This is where you must put your faith into operation. You must take action.

There have been many times in my life where I have "held the fort," but I didn't stay there. I did this one time while I lay in a bed and sat in a wheel chair. But I didn't just stay there on the defense. I allowed the Holy Spirit to comfort me, help me, intercede with me, stand by me, advocate for me, and strengthen me—and then I took action and walked out. I was set free from the broken bones and weakness that had held me down. Yes, there was protection, food, and fellowship during my time of holding fast. The walls of the hospital were like the walls of a fort. They helped to a certain degree, but I was not free. I received the strength to not only sit there, but also to get out and enjoy life!

An important point I don't want you to miss is this: *While I was "in the fort," I did not help very many people. However, when I got out, many were helped.*

My friend, if you are just holding on—just "holding the fort"— use your faith in the Lord by His Word. Then, allow the Holy Spirit to strengthen you to get up and walk out of the fort that has held you captive. You must allow the Holy Spirit to get involved. He will show you what words to use, how to say them, when to say them, and where to say them. He is your Commander. When He gives you orders, follow them. Meditate on the following scriptures so that you'll be ready to hear Him:

> *The LORD is my rock, and my fortress, and my deliverer; my God, my strength, in whom I will trust; my buckler, and the horn of my salvation, and my high tower* (Psalm 18:2).

The LORD is my light and my salvation; whom shall I fear? the LORD is the strength of my life; of whom shall I be afraid? (Psalm 27:1).

The LORD is my strength and my shield; my heart trusted in him, and I am helped: therefore my heart greatly rejoiceth; and with my song will I praise him (Psalm 28:7).

The LORD is their strength, and he is the saving strength of his anointed (Psalm 28:8).

God is our refuge and strength, a very present help in trouble (Psalm 46:1).

Because of his strength will I wait upon thee: for God is my defense (Psalm 59:9).

A wise man is strong; yea, a man of knowledge increaseth strength (Proverbs 24:5).

♦ ♦ ♦ ♦ ♦ ♦ ♦

The task before you is not greater than the force of God within you.

Another...: The Same Kind, but Different

9

OUR INTERCESSOR

It is amazing how much good coming to this part of this book is even doing for me. The Holy Spirit is using it to bring things to my attention that I need to step back into, things I was not doing as I ought. I had slipped and had begun letting people—and even the church—have an affect on my prayer life. All the while, I should have been affecting *them* with it. We are not supposed to be praying to be seen and heard of others. We are to pray and be seen of God. So, we might as well jump in with the Word and the Holy Spirit and "let it rip" in the Spirit, allowing the Holy Spirit to help us all the way.

Man has misused everything that God has done by His Word and with the Holy Spirit. *Although it is true that there is no limit to how far you can go with God, when you start trying to duplicate only the method in which He moves, you will get in trouble.* If you take the time to study all the things Jesus did in the Gospels, you will see that He did not do anything the same way twice. Yes, He healed more than once. He raised the dead more than once. He fed thousands more than once. He opened blind eyes more than once. The Spirit led Him more than once. He prayed more than once. The same principles were involved, but the methods were different each time. What were the principles? The following is a list of some of them:

1. Knowing God's Word.

2. Knowing the Father.

3. Having faith in Whom and what you know.

4. Praying continually.

5. Being led by the Holy Spirit.

6. Hearing what the Spirit says.

7. Believing what the Spirit says.

8. Doing what the Spirit says.

9. Doing it the way the Spirit says.

10. Doing it where the Spirit says.

11. Doing it as long as the Spirit says.

12. Doing it to bring glory to God and not for personal glory.

This chapter is about the Holy Spirit as our Intercessor. To have a better understanding of Him as our Intercessor, we need to understand what the words *intercede* and *intercessor* mean. An *intercessor* is "one that intercedes"—and we call this intercession. So, what are the meanings of these words? *Vine's Expository Dictionary of Biblical Words* (© 1985, Thomas Nelson) defines them as follows:

> *Intercession* is "a prayer, petition, or entreaty in favor of another."
> To *intercede* is "to light upon a person or a thing, to fall in with, to hit upon, a person or a thing; to fall in with, meet with in order to converse"; then, "to make

petition," especially "to make intercession, plead with a person," either for or against others.

Thayer's Greek Lexicon, Electronic Database (© 2000 by Biblesoft) defines *intercede* this way:

> To *intercede* is "to go to or meet a person, especially for the purpose of conversation, consultation, or supplication."

There are three key verses of Scripture that we need to look into as we learn more of the Holy Spirit as our Intercessor:

> *Likewise the Spirit also helpeth our infirmities: for we know not what we should pray for as we ought: but the Spirit itself maketh intercession for us with groanings which cannot be uttered. And he that searcheth the hearts knoweth what is the mind of the Spirit, because he maketh intercession for the saints according to the will of God* (Romans 8:26-27).

> *For he that speaketh in an unknown tongue speaketh not unto men, but unto God: for no man understandeth him; howbeit in the spirit he speaketh mysteries* (1 Corinthians 14:2).

One of the simplest ways to get the Holy Spirit to help you is to just simply ask Him for His help in that specific area. I do hope you know that you can ask God for anything that lines up with His Word and be assured of His response (1 John 5:14-15). There are some things you will need to make a demand on in the name of Jesus; there are some things you will need to receive by standing on Scripture; and there are things you will have to ask of the Holy Spirit.

Ask for His Help

I remember when my son Jason was still in diapers. One night, he awakened crying and screaming so loudly that it woke me up. My wife, Mary, said that it was the only time I ever woke up to help with Jason. It wasn't that I didn't want to help; it just so happens that I am a very sound sleeper. Anyhow, I got up to help: I fed him; I prayed in the name of Jesus; I sang songs; I walked the floor with him; and I patted him. But it seemed that the more I did, the harder and louder he cried. I mean, it was really bad.

I asked the Holy Spirit to reveal to me what the problem was and why Jason was crying like this. Then, I started praying in the Spirit. After praying in the Spirit for just a few minutes, I heard these words, "The diaper pin is sticking him. Snap it closed." Jason stopped crying just as fast as you could snap your finger. You see, I did not know how to pray about this in the beginning; but, as I prayed in the Spirit, the mystery of the problem was revealed.

The thing I did last was what I should have done first—simply ask Him for help. *When I asked for help, the Holy Spirit manifested with a good spoken word to effectively resolve the situation.*

If you are not getting the answers and help you need for your victory, save yourself a lot of time and energy and ask the Holy Spirit to help—and He will. You cannot tell Him how; but, if you desire for Him to manifest, He will. *He will help you set the stage for your answer to come forth.*

Let Him Help You Pray

One of the first times I remember asking the Holy Spirit to help me pray was after I had spent much time sharing with my father about his need to be born again. I shared with him. I preached to him. I prayed for him. It got to the point where I was tired of working the things of God that I knew to get him to receive Jesus as His Lord and Savior. So, one night I just stopped doing what I already knew and asked the Holy Spirit to help me.

Before I tell you what happened, let me point out something very important to you. Over the years that I have been in the ministry, there are reasons that I have seen very clearly that many people do not get the help and answers they need. When I do not get the help and answers I need, I have to stop what I'm doing, slow down my thinking, and ask myself, "On what or whom am I depending? Am I depending on the arm of the flesh? Am I depending on my experiences? Am I depending on someone else? Am I just depending on the confessions I like?" In other words, the first thing you should check is on what or whom you are depending for help.

Remember, in the beginning God did not just depend on Himself. He also depended on the Word and the Holy Spirit. So, after I had used up all I knew, I surrendered to the help of the Holy Spirit. I distinctly asked the Holy Spirit to help me and it started by me praying in the Spirit (Jude 1:20-25):

But ye, beloved, building up yourselves on your most holy faith, praying in the Holy Ghost, Keep yourselves in the love of God, looking for the mercy of our Lord Jesus Christ unto eternal life. And of some have compassion, making a difference: And others save with fear, pulling them out of the fire; hating even the garment spotted by the flesh. Now unto him that is able to keep you from falling, and to present you faultless before the presence of his glory with exceeding joy, To the only wise God our Saviour, be glory and majesty, dominion and power, both now and ever. Amen.

To understand what I am getting ready to share, you will need to remember what we have said about the Holy Spirit and His roles as Another Comforter, Helper, Counselor, Standby, Strengthener, and Advocate, as well as the definitions of *intercede.*

When the Holy Spirit started helping me pray, I was praying in tongues. After praying in tongues for a while, it seemed like someone just grabbed my arm and that we started marching strongly and heavily. Then, the next thing that happened was that I fell into a hole, which seemed to be just wide enough for me to slide down head first. In the natural, I would not have been able to turn around in this hole. It was tight, but slick. It was like someone had smeared oil on the sides of it so that I could not grasp the sides and stop myself. The hole felt more like a black steel pipe.

It seemed as though I was sliding down this pipe like a bullet. I was sliding down head first with my arms straight out in front of me. Then, I noticed that no one was holding my arm anymore. My eyes were wide open, but everything was dark. Then, I heard sounds that I had never heard before, sounds so loud and with such a pitch that I wanted to grab my ears—but, I couldn't, because the hole was too tight for me to get my hands back to my head.

Right after hearing those sounds, I started seeing flames. The flames were huge, and it seemed as though they had hands themselves and were trying to grab me. Just as soon as I saw these flames, two things happened at once—I mean, faster than you can blink your eye. First, I saw my father, and he was almost in the hands of the flames. Second, I felt someone grab my feet and snatch me out of that pipe. As soon as they grabbed my feet, I grabbed my father by the hands, as he had been sliding feet first. I saw his face, and it had an expression that was totally full of fear and begging for help. When the hands of the Holy Spirit grabbed me, and I grabbed my father, we came out of that pipe like a rocket!

This took place while I was at a prayer meeting with about eight other people at RHEMA Bible Training Center. There were people there who saw me and said that it looked to them as if I was wrestling a big boa constrictor. I said, "I didn't feel like I had been wrestling." Then, I asked, "How long did this take place?" They said, "For over one hour." To me it seemed like only five minutes. It was only a few months after this that my father received Jesus as his Lord and Savior.

What happened there was that the Holy Spirit was helping me pray for my father's deliverance. Yes, He let me see into the spirit realm. I saw the realm of Hell. I saw the darkness, and I saw the flames. I didn't mention this before, but I also heard people in the background crying and screaming for help.

Please understand. We don't always have to see into the spirit world or experience something like this to know that the Holy Spirit is helping us in our prayers. I will tell you this: you will know.

Use It Correctly

I am getting ready to relay something that could cause some people a problem. I don't mean it to be a problem, because it is the truth. Yes, I know people have gone "off the deep end" with all kinds of things that they called prayer or the Holy Spirit. You know, even the Devil gets blamed for things he did not do. God gets blamed for all kinds of horrible things that He didn't do. We all have been wrongly accused or misused. But, just because someone has misused the things of God, does not mean we are to back off from them.

For example, people have misused money. People have misused the automobile. People have misused the telephone. You name it, and people have misused it. But, that does not mean we should stop using money, automobiles, telephones, etc. What do we do? We must learn to use things correctly. Well, the same thing is true with the things of God—learn to use them correctly. So what if someone else misused them, it does not mean that you will.

Many people's lives at home, at church, and at work have become so programmed and pushed for time that the Holy Spirit is not even allowed the time to say, "Hello." He has the time for us, but we don't give Him our time like we should. Remember the chapter on fellowship? The Holy Spirit wants our fellowship, and we *need* His.

Use the teaching materials that God has made available to you to help you learn of Jesus and to renew your mind with His Word; but, *do not let anything take the place of the Word or the Other Comforter*, Who is the Holy Spirit.

When we ask the Holy Spirit to help us in anything, He makes available to us all the resources our heavenly Father has. Even though you may not understand something, your allowing the Holy Spirit to help you as you pray in tongues will cause the mind of God to be revealed to you in the area of your need. First Corinthians 14:2 (*AMP*) makes this very clear:

> *For one who speaks in an [unknown] tongue speaks not to men but to God, for no one understands or catches his meaning, because in the [Holy] Spirit he utters secret truths and hidden things [not obvious to the understanding].*

This verse not only applies to spiritual things, it applies to everything pertaining to life. Remember the story with Jason and the diaper pin? I could tell you hundreds of stories, but I'll leave it with just those two. The Holy Spirit is ready and willing to be your Intercessor. All you need do is ask Him.

◆◆◆◆◆◆◆

The Spirit of the LORD will rest on him—the Spirit of wisdom and of understanding, the Spirit of counsel and of power, the Spirit of knowledge and of the fear of the LORD (Isaiah 11:2, *NIV*).

Another...: The Same Kind, but Different

.

10

THE CALL AND THE SPIRIT

The call and cause will affect our attitude, authority, love, faith, finances, and the lives of others. Let us allow the Holy Spirit to obey His call and help us for God. The Holy Spirit longs to do it. There was a cause for his calling to be Another Comforter.

I want to give you some very important definitions to some key words. With these definitions in mind, think about the Holy Spirit as One called and chosen to help bring about actions that birth results. He can do this, because He has taken on the responsibility that goes with His calling. Just because someone was in heaven does not mean he or she will take on his or her God-given responsibilities. Lucifer did not, and he fell. The Holy Spirit has taken on His responsibilities. As you study these definitions, remember that the Holy Spirit is called to be our Helper and Comforter.

1. *Helper*: "a skilled worker helping another; to be of use to; to give assistant to; to make more bearable; benefit; change for the better; to help us restrain from doing something."

2. *Comfort*: "to support or to ease the pressure of."

3. *Partner*: "one who shares; one associated with another for action; as two people living together and sharing everything; to join or associate with another."

<u>4.</u> *General Partner* (not part-time): "a partner whose liability for partnership, debts, and obligations is unlimited and applicable to every member of a class, kind, or group and is not confined by specialization or limitations." (The Holy Spirit deals with both the universal and personal aspects of life.)

5. *Exploits*: "large-scale rapid, spectacular expansion; bursting out and bursting forth."

The number-one thing in our lives must be the Word of God. However, for us to completely understand that we need help—and one of the best ways to receive help—is to pray in the Spirit. *Praying the promises does not replace praying in the Spirit. Praying in the Spirit does not replace praying the promises. It takes both working together.* Remember, when you approach the Father, the Word, and the Holy Spirit, purpose in your heart and mind as to why you want their attention. You do it with people, so apply it here.

Why Pray in the Spirit?

In the last day, that great day of the feast, Jesus stood and cried, saying, If any man thirst, let him come unto me, and drink. He that believeth on me, as the scripture hath said, out of his belly shall flow rivers of living water. (But this spake he of the Spirit, which they that believe on him should receive: for the Holy Ghost was not yet given; because that Jesus was not yet glorified.) (John 7:37-39).

Notice Jesus said "rivers," not "river." There are many rivers, and praying in the Spirit is just one of them. Joy is a river. Praise is a river. Worship is a river. Giving is a river. Praying is a river. Speaking forth the Word is a river. Forgiveness is a river. Repentance is a river. Laughter is a river. Dancing before the Lord is a river. *It is praying in the Spirit that will help you to release these rivers.*

Remember, praying in the Spirit is the only supernatural thing you can do whenever you want to, for as long as you want to, and where you want to. "Lord, help our want-tos!" Following, I have made a list of 28 reasons for praying in the Spirit:

1. Jesus said that we should (Mark 16:17).

2. God said that He would speak to His people this way (Isaiah 28:11).

3. It is restful and refreshing (Isaiah 28:12).

4. Doing so enables you to talk to God without the Devil's knowing what you are saying (1 Corinthians 14:2).

5. It edifies and builds you up (1 Corinthians 14:4; Jude 1:20).

6. Praying in the Spirit helps you pray and sing (1 Corinthians 14:14-15).

7. It is the best way to give thanks (1 Corinthians 14:16-17).

8. It serves as a sign to those who do not believe (1 Corinthians 14:22).

9. It helps keep you to remain in faith (Jude 1:20).

10. It keeps you in love of God (Jude 1:21).

11. Praying in the Spirit helps you walk in compassion (Jude 1:22).

12. It also helps to keep you from falling (Jude 1:24).

13. It makes you more aware of His presence with joy (Jude 1:24).

14. Praying in the Holy Spirit releases rivers (John 7:37-39).

15. It also releases healing (Ezekiel 47:8-9).

16. And, it releases blessings (Ezekiel 47:10, 12).

17. Praying in the Spirit releases growth (Ezekiel. 47:12).

18. It also makes you more aware of His presence (John 14:16-17).

19. It aids your being filled with the Spirit, causing you to be Spirit possessed (Ephesians 5:18-20; Acts 2:15).

20. It helps you to build up others by releasing grace (Colossians 3:16).

21. Praying in the Spirit helps you release fruit (Galatians 5:22-25).

22. Doing this also helps you draw from the seven spiritual facets of God (Isaiah 11:1-3).

23. It aids your having the judgments of God (Isaiah 11:3).

24. It helps you walk in the things of the Kingdom (Romans 14:17).

25. Praying this way helps your praying (Romans 8:26-27).

26. Praying in the Holy Spirit reveals the mind of God to you (Romans 8:26-27).

27. It helps you in your weakness to bring you through (Romans 8:26-27).

28. It helps you sow and reap in the Spirit (Galatians 6:8).

Another...: The Same Kind, but Different

A FINAL WORD

You can be of good cheer, for Jesus calls you. You are called: to be His child; to be full of the Spirit; to be righteous; and to be holy. You are also called: to be healed; to be prosperous; to be a fisher of men; to preach; to lay hands on the sick; and to cast out devils. And finally, you are called: to grow up; to give; to love; to forgive; to go into the entire world; and to pray.

The list could go on. I used the word *call,* when most of these are commandments. Yet, when you are commanded to do something, it is like a strong call. You still have to make a decision to respond to the command or call. It is your responsibility, so take it. The Holy Spirit will help you if you will ask and let Him.

Accept the call and the responsibility that goes with it. When a person is called, it means a request or demand has been made for the person to be summoned to a particular activity or position. But, after the call, the person will need to be chosen.

For example, we are all called to become children of God. We could say that we want to be children of God, but you will not be chosen until you respond to the call correctly and personally. You do this by believing in your heart that Jesus is the Son of

God and that God raised Him from the dead. You believe it so strongly that you say it. Only then you are chosen.

There are many reasons behind your responding to the call of being a child of God. One of them is so that you may testify of the truth about the Father, the Son (the Word), and the Holy Spirit. The results being that you stay free and lead others to freedom.

For each and every call, there is a cause. When there is a cause, it is the motivation for action that brings about results. When we stand for a cause, we become agents for that cause. Keep in mind that God did not call us to be secret agents (hiding our purpose), nor did God call us to be double agents (wavering in our loyalties). We are to boldly follow the call and keep our focus on following the One Who called us.

For you to carry out the call that God has given you, you must take the responsibilities that go with your particular call. This means that you will be in a position of accountability. As you choose to walk in the calling you've been given, you will have Another Comforter with you all the way.

♦ ♦ ♦ ♦ ♦ ♦ ♦

God is faithful, by whom ye were called unto the fellowship of his Son Jesus Christ our Lord (1 Corinthians 1:9).

Faithful is he that calleth you, who also will do it (1 Thessalonians 5:24).

And I thank Christ Jesus our Lord, who hath enabled me, for that he counted me faithful, putting me into the ministry... (1 Timothy 1:12).

The Father has a call.
The Lord Jesus has a call.
The Word has a call.
The Holy Spirit has a call.
The angels have a call.
The Devil has a call.
We are called
so that we can accomplish
what we are called to do.

We must cooperate with the Father, the Lord Jesus, the Word, the Holy Spirit, and our brother and sisters in Christ so that they can do what they are called to do. We must not cooperate with the Devil. Do not hinder the Father, the Son (the Word), the Holy Spirit, the angels, others or yourself from walking in the call of God.

Another…: The Same Kind, but Different

SIGNS, WONDERS, AND MIRACLES

Jesus said that we should do the works He did and that signs and wonders would follow those who believe. I am a believer.

Verily, verily, I say unto you, He that believeth on me, the works that I do shall he do also; and greater works than these shall he do; because I go unto my Father (John 14:12).

And these signs shall follow them that believe; In my name shall they cast out devils; they shall speak with new tongues; They shall take up serpents; and if they drink any deadly thing, it shall not hurt them; they shall lay hands on the sick, and they shall recover (Mark 16:17-18).

Following are brief descriptions of just two of the many things my wife and I have seen God do. Although we've seen numerous miracles ranging from people being delivered and born again and many healed of disease, infirmity, and injury to those who were raised from the dead, these particular testimonies are listed here as evidence of the wonderful benefits of heeding the leading of the Holy Spirit. It is a great honor and blessing to have a wife like I have, one with whom I can walk hand-in-hand, doing the works of Jesus. She has been and remains involved with all the things the Lord is doing as we continue our walk together with Him. Thank you, Mary, for being who you are.

The Wild Child

I want to share with you something that happened one night, because it covers many of the things we've been discussing. Also, what took place that night had a major impact on the town where we lived at the time. Many were added to the family of God as a result.

We were living in Kalibo, Aklan, where we had a Bible school. We lived there for over eight years. Many times in Kalibo, as in most of the Philippines, there are periods when there is no electricity. The power would just go out without warning. This was one of those times.

Mary and I were upstairs in our apartment, sleeping. At exactly 1:00 a.m., we heard a motorcycle drive up directly in front of our place. It stopped on the street, only about five feet from our front door. Because of the complete blackout, we could clearly see the light of the motorcycle as it shone into our home. I got up and looked out of the window. I saw two people on the motorcycle, a man and a woman. I did not recognize the man, but I did recognize the woman. She had been to our house before, bringing sick people for prayer. I went downstairs and opened the door.

Before I could even say a word, they started in excitedly, "Brother James, Brother James— come, come! We need your help."

I asked, "What do you want me to do to help you?"

The man said, "Brother James, it is my baby. No man can tame him. The baby is wild. The baby is screaming like a wild cat, and no one can touch him. He even threw my wife out of the bed!"

"What?" I asked, somewhat surprised. "How can a baby throw a woman out of a bed? How old is your baby?"

The father said, "Two years old."

I found out later that his wife weighed about 140 pounds, and the two-year-old had picked her up and dropped her out of the bed—this was witnessed by 10 people. Please note that this was not accomplished through the physical strength of this baby; it was the result of demonic influence and empowerment.

By this time I was wide-awake. The man and woman were still saying, 'Come, Brother James, come!"

I said, "I'll come" and began praying in tongues.

I didn't pray in tongues just to be praying. I was preparing my mind and heart. I was praying in tongues to draw from the Holy Spirit to give me counsel, to help me, to strengthen me, to stand-by me, to be my Advocate, and even to comfort me. I needed Him to guide me and lead me in what to do in this time of need.

I went upstairs, leaned over Mary and said, "I am going to pray for someone. I'll be back in 30 minutes."

She said, "Sure, I've heard that before! Good night, James!"

I got on my motorcycle and followed them into the totally black night. We went through a part of town that I recognized, then to a place I didn't recognize. We turned down an alley next to the highway department.

The next thing I saw were bamboo huts along with some grass huts. There were a lot of them quite close together. We stopped about 15 feet from one. About 20 people had gathered around this little two-room hut.

I followed the man into his house. As I got to the front door, I saw something I had only seen once before. There were human skulls mounted on each side of the front door with all kinds of little things hung over them. I had seen this one other time where I saw about 15 human skulls mounted on top of a fence post on the side of the highway up in the mountains. I started praying in tongues as fast as I could.

We went into the house. There were all sorts of animal skins hanging from the ceilings and walls. About the time I saw all these things, I heard a cry from the other room. It sounded just like a bobcat. This cry was coming from the baby!

I had been hunting before and had heard a bobcat caught by a pack of dogs. It couldn't get away, so it just started screaming. That is exactly what this baby sounded like.

The woman who had brought the father to my house had interpreted for me before, so I asked her to interpret for me now. Then I continued praying in tongues.

She asked, "Brother James, what are you going to do?' (I noticed she did not ask, "What are *we* going to do," but, "What are *you* going to do?") I said, " I am going to pray," and I continued praying.

About 10 seconds later, the Holy Spirit started showing Himself to be just Who Jesus said He would be, and He began moving. He started comforting me, helping me, standing by me, and strengthening me. He started given me the ability to witness and do the works of Jesus.

The first thing the Holy Spirit asked me to do was to ask everyone to leave the room. I started around the room with the interpreter, asking each one to leave. Everything was going very smoothly until I reached the mother. I asked her to leave the room, and she exploded in my face.

"Brother James, I am not going to leave my baby. I am not leaving my baby." She said it again and again, louder and louder. She even grabbed me by the shoulders and started shaking me.

I looked her straight in the eyes. With a very loud voice, I said, "If you want Jesus to heal your baby, you had better get out NOW."

Just as quickly as I said it, she calmed down and said in such a gentle way, "Yes, sir, Brother James."

All of a sudden, it was just the baby, the interpreter, and I. Plus the Holy Ghost—oh, don't forget the Standby!

I looked up. In the left corner, the baby was screaming in the bed, and in the opposite corner was the interpreter, looking like she had been shot out of a cannon into another world! She just kept saying over and over, "Brother James, what are you going to do now?"

I said, "Pray, pray."

As I was praying, I walked over to the baby, and picked him up. The baby was still screaming and kicking. Then the Holy Ghost said, *"Give the baby a spanking on his back side."*

I said, "No. They don't spank babies in this country. It is against their custom."

The Holy Spirit said, *"I know that. Why do you think I wanted everyone out of the room?"*

I said, " Praise God!" Spanking this child was just what I wanted to do anyhow! (Please note: if I had done that because of my own thinking, I would have gotten in trouble. It takes the Holy Spirit's wisdom to accomplish in the proper way what needs to be done.)

I turned the child over and gave him three good, solid swats on his backside. Then there was total silence. Not a sound. I looked down at the baby. There was no movement. Then I heard a voice saying, "You have killed the baby. You have killed the baby." These words came just as fast as lightning.

I looked down on the child, wondering what to do next. I turned the child face up. I then saw the greatest miracle I have ever seen: the child opened his eyes, and I heard him say in perfect English, "Jesus loves me and Mommy and Daddy."

I was so happy that I almost threw the baby in the air! The interpreter started dancing for joy. The mother came in and began jumping up and down. The father came in and started hugging me.

After things settled down, I told them they needed to become born again and to get rid of all the evil witchcraft items and burn them. That night, 15 people were born again and filled with the Spirit, praying in the Holy Ghost.

As I rode back to my house, I looked in the rearview mirror of my Honda 250 and saw a huge fire with the Devil's tools being burned. Hallelujah! Thank God for the Holy Spirit, my Helper, Standby, and Strengthener.

Within the next week, many families and children were delivered and born again as a result of the Holy Spirit's manifesting Himself. And guess what? When I arrived back home, I had been gone only 30 minutes!

What to Do When You've Missed It

Have you ever had the inward witness to do something, yet you did not do it—and then wish you had? We have all probably done this before. Well, if you have, there is a way to correct it and still get the victory. The way is the way of the Spirit, based on the Word.

Have you ever thought about the fact that failure to do what you know the Holy Spirit said to do is a sin? Why? Because your failure to obey the Spirit demonstrates a lack of trust that is not of faith—and anything that is not of faith is sin (Romans 14:23).

Notice that I said that the way to correct this is the way of the Spirit, based on the Word. Why am I saying it this way? Because the Holy Spirit only sponsors the Word.

While we were living in the Philippines, we had many visitors come. I had a specific situation take place when one of my best friends came to visit. I owned a very good motorcycle that was made available to me by the people who supported us. One afternoon, I let my friend use the bike. When he returned, he parked it just outside the front door of our house.

I mean, it was only eight feet from the front door, but there was a fence between the bike and the front entrance. The fence was there for a purpose, not just for looks. It was there to help protect what was ours. There had been times in the past in which I left things outside, and all was okay the next day. But this day was different.

That night when we went to bed—just as soon as I put by head on the pillow—the Holy Spirit said, *"Go move the bike."*

I lay there saying, "It will be okay. The angels will watch over it. They have done it before they will do it again." So I just went to sleep.

The next morning, the motorcycle was gone. I felt like kicking myself. Just think about it: all I had to do to move the bike was go downstairs, open the gate, and put it in the driveway behind the fence. I measured it—it was 28 steps one way. But no, my flesh wanted to rest. It was tired.

So, I called the police and the army and told them that my motorcycle was gone. I posted a reward. I even paid for the travel and food for these guys to look for it, but they could not find it. It was found later in two pieces in two separate places and only after much money had been spent. Isn't that a sad thing? All because I did not obey a simple request of the Holy Spirit to go move the bike! Thank God that all our failures to obey are not so costly.

I do need to tell you that the boy who stole the bike was on drugs, but he and his mother came to my office and asked forgiveness. I forgave him and prayed for him.

Even so, this still left me with no bike. I was stumped as to how to get back what the Devil stole, knowing that it was because of my being in the flesh and not obeying the Holy Spirit. Well, I asked the Holy Spirit to help me—after I had asked Jesus to forgive me, asked my wife to forgive me, forgiven myself, and forgiven my friend for leaving it outside. It was not his fault anyhow. It was my bike. It was my responsibility. The Holy Spirit tried to help me carry out my responsibility, but I did not cooperate.

The first thing you must do when you miss it is to be honest with those involved, admit you missed it, and asked forgiveness. First, talk to the Father, Jesus, and the Holy Spirit; then you must listen to the instructions on how to correct what happened. Most people just asked for forgiveness and go on their way. If you really want the victory, go all the way until it takes place.

So, I had asked forgiveness. Then what? As I was praying, the Holy Spirit said, *"Write a letter to those who helped you get the bike, and tell them exactly what happened."*

I said, "What? They will think I am careless and lazy, too lazy to go down stairs. They may even stop supporting us." But Praise the Lord, I wrote the letter, gave the complete details, and told them just how much I needed a bike for the Lord's work.

After mailing the letter to the 10 people the Holy Spirit had told me to write, all the money needed to replace the bike was given. Each person I wrote to gave some money to help. When all was said and done, it covered every dollar that was needed to purchase a new bike. Not only a new bike, but also an even bigger and better bike.

* * * * *

The key is listening to the simple directions of the Holy Spirit and obeying them in detail. You can do it to keep from suffering loss and defeat, and you can do it to get back what was lost and not remain defeated.

PRAYER

" *F*ather, I thank You for the person who has just read this book. If this person does not know You as Lord and Savior, I pray he or she will call on the name of Jesus and be saved. If this individual is your child, but has not yet received the Baptism in the Holy Spirit with the evidence of speaking in tongues, I pray for him or her to receive. And Father, I ask the Holy Spirit to manifest Himself the way He needs to for this person's benefit. It is my prayer that this reader allows the Word of God and the Holy Spirit free reign in his or her life and that he or she becomes and does all that You desire. Thank You, Jesus, for hearing this prayer and for honoring Your Word in this book. Amen."

Please let us hear from you about how this book has been a blessing to your life. Thank you!

James A. Rushton Ministries, Inc.
P.O. Box 256
Ocean Gate, NJ 08740-0256 USA
Email: jar@cfaith.com

Another...: The Same Kind, but Different

ABOUT THE AUTHOR

James A. Rushton has been sharing Jesus with others ever since he became born again in 1969. An alumnus from its beginning, James graduated from RHEMA Bible Training Center (RHEMA) in 1977 and was ordained by Kenneth E. Hagin.

In December of 1977, the Holy Spirit led James to Virginia where he met the Mary, who would later become his wife. After they were married, they went back to RHEMA where James completed a second year's curriculum, and Mary finished her first year. In 1981, the same year in which they graduated, they moved to the Philippines where they served as missionaries for over 12 years. While there, they adopted their son, Jason.

Between the two of them, James and his wife have ministered throughout the United States, the Philippines, Brazil, and Indonesia. They have seen every miracle in the book of Acts manifested—they have witnessed those who were lame, walk; the blind, see; the deaf hear; the dead raised up; and people delivered from all kinds of demonic oppression. Many have come to know Jesus as their Lord and Savior and have received the Baptism in the Holy Spirit.

James, Mary, and Jason are active members of Abundant Grace Church in Toms River, New Jersey, pastored by Anthony and

Carol Storino. James and Mary both teach in the School of the Bible. James regularly teaches evangelism, and Mary teaches in the Children's Church. James and Mary are available to teach and minister wherever the doors open.

"It is for your sake that I talk and walk like Jesus in word, in power, in the Holy Spirit, and with much assurance."